EBB AND FLOW
PART I
THE LIFE JOURNEY OF NOEL CADASSE

*The Authorized Biography
of Entrepreneur, Politician,
and Philanthropist Noel Cadasse*

Belleville, Ontario, Canada

EBB AND FLOW (PART I)
Copyright © 2013, Noel Cadasse

All Rights Reserved. No part of this publication may be reproduced, stored in a retrieval system or transmitted in any form or by any means—electronic, mechanical, photocopy, recording or any other—except for brief quotations in printed reviews, without the prior permission of the author.

ISBN: 978-1-4600-0200-1
LSI Edition: 978-1-4600-0201-8
E-book ISBN: 978-1-4600-0202-5
(E-book available from the Kindle Store, KOBO and the iBookstore)

Cataloguing data available from Library and Archives Canada

To order additional copies, visit:
www.essencebookstore.com

Guardian Books is an imprint of *Essence Publishing*, a Christian Book Publisher dedicated to furthering the work of Christ through the written word.
For more information, contact:
20 Hanna Court, Belleville, Ontario, Canada K8P 5J2
Phone: 1-800-238-6376 • Fax: (613) 962-3055
Email: info@essence-publishing.com
Web site: www.essence-publishing.com

Printed in Canada
by

DEDICATION

To my beautiful wife, Julia

Contents

Acknowledgements 7
Author's Notes 9
Foreword...11
Prologue..15
PART ONE: NOEL CADASSE: THE MAN AND HIS LIFE LESSONS
Chapter One: The Rhythm of the Life 21
Chapter Two: To Dream, to Conquer Life's Obstacles 23
Chapter Three: Life in Saint Lucia..25
Chapter Four: The Emigrant Longing 29
Chapter Five: Perspective of Success..31
Chapter Six: The Path of Peace 35
Chapter Seven: The Political Allure...39
Chapter Eight: Reaching for a Dream..43
Chapter Nine: Society Needs Safety Nets..47
Chapter Ten: The Fall and Forgiveness..49
Chapter Eleven: The Dream of the Man...51
Chapter Twelve: Birthday Reflections..55
Chapter Thirteen: A History of the Man 57
Chapter Fourteen: Discipline Shapes Character..................................61
Chapter Fifteen: The Simple Rhythm of Life......................................63
Chapter Sixteen: The Vision of the Man...67

Chapter Seventeen: The Political Experience 71
Chapter Eighteen: The Afflictions of the Man 75
Chapter Nineteen: How the Troubles Began 81
Chapter Twenty: Concluding Thoughts 85
Chapter Twenty-one: Concluding Advice 91
Chapter Twenty-two: Reflecting on My Life Lessons 97

PART TWO: MY VISION FOR SOCIETY'S DEVELOPMENT

Chapter Twenty-three: Inaugural Speech 103
Chapter Twenty-four: Tourism Association Speech 109
Chapter Twenty-five: Political Speech, Vieux Fort 125
Chapter Twenty-six: Advice for Saint Lucia 131
Chapter Twenty-seven: Hospitality Industry Speech 135
Chapter Twenty-eight: AgriTour Speech 147
Chapter Twenty-nine: Political Speech 155
Chapter Thirty: Tourism and Agriculture 161

PART THREE: PHOTOS

Desiderata 179

ACKNOWLEDGEMENTS

How can I begin to write an acknowledgement of thanks and appreciation to the countless people who have contributed to a life as rich in experience as mine? I have so many people who have shaped my destiny, who toiled long and hard for my comfort and my achievements. Indeed, I have stood on the shoulders of giants who have contributed so much to my life. With the deepest of gratitude and humility in my heart, I thank everyone who crossed my path in life.

First, I thank God, whose grace through the Lord Jesus Christ brought me salvation and sustained me in the times I felt despair. The Lord has always been gracious and kind to me, blessing me above and beyond what I deserve.

To my adorable wife, Julia, thank you for all your years of faithful support, nurture, love, and care. Without you, my life could not be so fruitful. I owe you an eternal gratitude.

To my children: Ricky, Joycie, Ross, Kervin, Candace, Sharnell, Noel Jr., Liza, and Juli-Anne—thank you for growing up to be decent human beings. I am proud of you all.

To Pastor Emmanuel McLaurens, who prayed with me and my family and counselled us in our most trying time—I will never forget your kind love towards us; to Pastor Dudley Mayers, who always made himself available to me whenever I needed his advice; and to the following wonderful people who have contributed to my life in remarkable ways: Sister Babsie, Sister Trim, Marva Tyndale, Cletus Springer, Fedelis Trim, Cletus Charlmagne, Shaun Michael Samaroo, Mary Popo, Andrew Frederick, Steven Andre, Guy Mayers, Nicholas John, Willie James, Frank Giraud, Dr. Alphonsius St. Rose, Claire Ceromain, George Theophilus, and, posthumously my mother, Eudoxia Cadasse, my father, George Cadasse, William Edgecomb, McMillan Andrew, and Romanus Lausiquot. Also to everyone who has supported me in one way or another and contributed to the shaping of my destiny—thank you all for your contributions in the shaping of the life story that is told in this book.

Last, but by no means least, I extend my profound thanks and appreciation to the prime minister of Saint Lucia, Dr. Kenny Anthony, and to a leader of exceptional conscientiousness, Mr. Leo Clarke.

Author's Notes

This book is a synopsis of the life I lived over the past sixty years. In writing a biography, one is tempted to look back on life with one of several attitudes: a deep sense of nostalgia; an arrogance and pride for the achievements; a sense of failure because of the human weaknesses to which we are prone in this world; or gratitude and thankfulness for a life well-lived.

I publish my life story here, albeit just a synopsis, with a sense of intense gratitude and thankfulness for the journey I have been through. I feel fortunate and blessed that I have traversed this earth for these many years. I made many mistakes. I could have done a lot of things better. With hindsight, one is tempted to fall into despair. But I want to clutch at the things I am happy for, the moments that shaped the path that resulted in me being the person I am today.

Through this journey, I have gathered some understanding and wisdom of the reality of life. This nugget of information I want to share with the world, especially the younger generations comprising my children and grandchildren. This book accomplishes that goal. I write this biography because I believe everyone learns something of value from living this life. And that diamond of valuable knowledge, of seeing the world uniquely as an individual who never was before and never will be again, should not be lost. I would have every person pass on what they have learned about life to future generations and to their world.

Writing this book itself has been a journey. The journey has been a microcosm of life itself—happy and euphoric at times, frustrating and hard at other times. Many times I have felt like giving up. This book has been nearly three years in the writing. It truly has been a labour, and I would like to believe it is a labour of love.

I am thankful that I could have persevered and exercised patience to see this day, when the writing is done and the publishing is over with. Now on to the

EBB AND FLOW

job of circulating it: I want this work to live on long after I am gone, to conquer the harsh reality of time and become a monumental work of immortality. Of course, that is asking for too much. But I have lived my life like that—always asking for too much, reaching too far out. Yet, isn't that what constitutes the joy of living? That we can stretch ourselves to the limit of our human creativity, our potential as created in us by the Creator?

I have lived a full life. I have loved every moment of it, even those moments when I felt the excruciating pain of being human—when, for example, I lay in bed in hospital waiting for a quadruple bypass heart surgery. Looking back, I know that even that moment was a chapter in this life I have lived—a chapter to be digested and accepted and analyzed for the crucial life lesson it offers.

I hope, dear reader, that you would be kind to me as you read this book, that you would approach it with the idea of seeing what insight you can gain from my life journey, to make yours that much more valuable, that much more appreciated and cherished.

One thing I learned from this labour of love—life moves in ebbs and flows, with a rhythm to which we can either choose to dance or fight. I chose to dance to the rhythm of life. And when I got too tired, I had the stability of loving people in my life to catch me whenever I would fall.

Enjoy this book. I offer it to you, this glimpse into the deepest recess of my heart, with the hope that my life can light the path of yours a little brighter.

The book is divided into three sections: Part One is the narrative of my life story—a brief look at the lessons I have learned along the journey and some of the key incidents that shaped the pathway of that journey. Part Two is a documenting of speeches I gave over the course of my life as a senior Caribbean politician and businessman. These speeches outline my vision and my agendas and my crusades. They illustrate what I have lived for and fought for, how I have used my time on this earth to make life easier and better for the society into which I was born. Part Three comprises the conclusion and my thoughts on this life.

Noel Cadasse
September, 2009
Toronto, Ontario, Canada

FOREWORD

Noel Cadasse is a striking personality, commanding and authoritative in his bearing. When I first met him, he was manager of a business establishment in Toronto, Ontario, Canada. His presence in the office as we first talked was imposing and almost intimidating. He is literally a giant of a man. A first meeting with this man is bound to be memorable.

It is, however, as a friendship develops that one becomes aware of the depth of the man's character. After only a few weeks of knowing him, I wanted as a young man to reach out for his mentorship, his guidance, his advice and leadership. In my early teenage life I have known two mentors. After I met Cadasse when I was in my late thirties, I added a third to my list. We have become such close friends over the past three years.

A remarkable fact about Cadasse is that meeting him never leaves a person the same. He touches lives, shaping and moulding destinies. Most people who meet him as business associates end up drawing close to him. He develops friendships easily. Yet, he is a demanding person: he does not leave people as he finds them. Instead he works and pushes people around him to aim higher in life, to reach beyond their comfort zones, to believe in their ability to accomplish.

It has been my distinct privilege to know this man. I write this foreword for his biography with immense gratitude and pride that he has become my friend. I have come to know his family, especially his adorable wife, Julia, a woman who has demonstrated remarkable patience, kindness, and compassion in her life. From this couple I have learned that life is a long, bumpy, winding road. From them, I have learned to live with patience and longsuffering and seeing the big picture.

Cadasse has not had an easy life. He has overcome incredible odds and achieved such astonishing feats that anyone who takes the time to reflect on his life would be instructed well on how to build their life. His life story is inspiring, instructive, and a wonderful lesson of the potential of the human being to conquer the obstacles stacked against an individual as he or she strives for success in this life.

I had the joy of visiting the Caribbees Hotel that he built in Saint Lucia and his sprawling home in the luxury Rodney Bay area. The hotel is a feat of incredible vision and classic taste. Situated on a mountain top overlooking the spectacular beach and acres and acres of palm trees, the hotel is a monument to the immense grandeur of a man's dream. To have been born in a poor village to poverty-stricken parents, to be forced to work at the age of sixteen, to have to fight his way through life from a teenager, to be able to become a senator in the Saint Lucian parliament, to open the first national insurance company in his country, and to develop a vision for his country's future—and even the future of the Caribbean—indeed stands as a monument to the depth of character inherent in this human being.

What is impressive about Noel is his determination, perseverance, optimism, faith in God, devotion to being a father to his children and a husband to his wife—to being a family man—and his strength of character to overcome any obstacle.

He has fallen many times in his life; he has faced enormous challenges in his businesses, political life, and personal health. But always, he has risen above it all to declare that circumstances need not dictate a person's life, that a man can take the future in his hands and accomplish much, that anyone can dream big dreams and achieve them.

For my own life, Noel has taught me the lessons of perseverance, believing in my dream, patience, the value of family, and the vital lesson that there is no such thing as an ordinary person. He was born a poor boy playing marbles on the shores of the Caribbean Sea. He became a senior statesman, business executive, compassionate philanthropist, and international diplomat.

His story is simply the little boy from a poor village who became a senator of the Saint Lucian parliament, and the journey that shaped his destiny, character, and achievements. His story is the story of the indomitable nature of the human spirit, triumphing despite it all. In Noel's life, the world can learn the art of achieving big dreams.

Shaun Michael Samaroo
Toronto, Ontario, Canada
September, 2009

"Our visions begin with our desires."

—Audre Lorde

prologue

MY PREAMBLE

Among the nations of the earth, sitting atop twin mountains like splendid sapphires decorating the sky blue Caribbean Sea, Saint Lucia stands as a modern wonder.

With two Nobel laureates among its citizens, with a glittering tourism package for the leisure of the world's vacationers, and with a people peaceful and progressive, the country models a marvellous, enchanting charm in its national character.

Leading such a nation calls for men and women of noble character. To become the premiere Saint Lucian citizen, to take on the responsibility for creating and generating a visionary developmental model, calls for leaders of exceptional conscientiousness and deep thoughtfulness.

These thoughts played in my mind as the new twenty-first century approached us, towards the end of the 1990s.

Born and raised in a little village in this grand and exquisite vacation paradise, I had grown up to become one of the nation's more successful businessmen and a community leader.

My family, contributing enormously to the private sector economy of the new nation, established solid marks on the consciousness of the people. We became household names in the land.

My wife, Julia, as a teacher, played a crucial role in shaping the early development of many of her students, now outstanding Saint Lucian citizens.

My children, products of the local education system, grew up with the unique Saint Lucian culture, accent, and ways of being.

I was the quintessential Saint Lucian, standing in a place of incredible blessings and full of hope for the promise of the new century. Our country surely would consolidate and become a gem of a nation in the new global village. It was an exciting time for me to be a Saint Lucian.

But not all was well in the nation's soul.

Our national hero and statesman extraordinaire, Sir John Compton, was getting advanced in age, and people were talking of the dearth of quality political leaders to fill the mammoth void his absence would create.

The search was on all over the world, including the US and England, for someone with the calibre of character that was required, in whose hands we could place the reins of our nation.

I happened to be in England on a business trip, and while attending a Saint Lucian function, I encountered a young Kenny Anthony, who was then a Saint Lucian law student in London.

Anthony impressed me from the start. I thought not only was he a bright and astute young man, but he also exhibited such passion, such a heartfelt concern for our nation. The natural thing for me to do was to ask him to come back home and serve. I did, thinking if he entered the political arena, our nation would be in good hands.

I went so far as to promise the young Anthony that I would join his team and work along with him to make sure he not only got into government but made a significant difference in preparing our nation for the new world. Happily, Dr. Kenny Anthony turned his back on a lucrative career overseas and returned home to Saint Lucia. Though at first not finding it as easy as we would all have liked, he persevered and stuck to the goal of making a difference.

I am happy to say that we developed a very good relationship, and I personally was privileged to be there when he needed a hand now and again. I believed in this leader, and I did my very best to make sure he was stable and ready for the road ahead.

Since I was a successful businessman in the nation at that time, I was in a solid position to reach out and offer him a hand when he needed it. I did so willingly, with a heart of love and care towards him.

This book, *Ebb and Flow*, chronicles my business and political ups and downs as a Saint Lucian citizen.

As the current prime minister, Dr. Kenny Anthony plays a dynamic and vital role in the events that have shaped my life. In parts of this book, I have written the historical situation as it unfolded between him and I, many times to my disadvantage. Sometimes it was necessary to be a bit critical of his leadership.

My Preamble

But I want to express how grateful I am for all Dr. Anthony did for my life and career as a politician. He graciously appointed me as a senator of the Saint Lucian parliament and thus paved the way for my role in the history of my nation. It is because of him that I am listed in the annals of history as a political leader of my country. As a senator, I spoke many times in parliament and enjoyed the accolades and privileges that came with the position. My role in the history of Saint Lucia through the senate could not have been possible without the generous kindness of Prime Minister Dr. Kenny Anthony.

The governor general of Saint Lucia received the recommendation from Prime Minister Anthony for me to be appointed senator in the upper house of the parliament. It was a gesture of profound meaning for me, for I had grown up a poor boy in a tiny village on the edge of the vast sea, and to be appointed to such a lofty position was a dream of unimaginable beauty.

I and my children and generations to come will forever cherish the faith Dr. Anthony, the governor general, and the nation embedded in my leadership ability.

After I had served my term as senator, Dr. Anthony again graciously appointed me as the first ever chairman of the National Gaming Board, a national body that shaped policies affecting the vital tourism industry and the gaming industry in the country. To boost my leadership in that role, Dr. Anthony, as prime minister, paved the way for me to complete relevant studies at the University of Nevada.

Through this appointment, I was privileged to shape the history of Saint Lucia by setting up the groundwork and foundation for the national gaming industry, a critical aspect of the tourism sector. As I was also president of the Hotel and Tourism Association, my role saw the nation develop the necessary system for tourism to be further entrenched as a major driver of the national economy.

In this life, one encounters defining souls, people who make a symbolic mark on one's life. Such has been Dr. Kenny Anthony's role in my life.

Such also has been the contribution of Leo Clarke to my life. Clarke served as the secretary of the Saint Lucia Labour Party, of which Dr. Anthony served as leader and myself as acting chairman during the ground-breaking national elections that saw Dr. Anthony become Saint Lucia's prime minister. Our party swept the elections in a landslide victory, winning all but one seat in parliament.

Despite never holding any kind of discussion with Mr. Leo Clarke, I learned through others that he was exceptionally kind and generous in my favour during the years of turmoil that erupted around me, as chronicled in this book. During my crisis, I believe Mr. Clarke made a significant and tremendous contribution to my well-being, to see that I would not be swept under the weight of my troubles. Acting purely out of the goodness of his heart, with even a thank-you letter to me for my contribution to the national affairs of Saint Lucia, Mr. Clarke acted out of his good conscience, out of the purity of his heart as a man of character and integrity and compassion. He used his influence to contribute to my life in a profound and lasting way.

I also remember with great fondness the camaraderie and brotherliness of my fellow parliamentarians. Despite heated debates and political differences in the house, when we socialized in the lobby or rubbed shoulders outside of the public platform, we enjoyed solid, cordial, and friendly relations. I forever will cherish those memories.

More than just chronicling my life journey, this book seeks to encourage and motivate readers with the lessons I have learned in my path through this world. Moving from the small fishing village of Anse La Raye, a farming community facing the ebb and flow of the massive blue Caribbean Sea and backing on to the rising mountains of the land, I grew up poor, working at a young age to help support my widowed mother.

So this book has a distinct purpose: to share with the world, to chronicle, engage, and contribute the life lessons I have learned in my journey. When my grandchildren and great-grands grow up, my story will not be lost to them, washed away by the sands of time. They can look into these pages and see their lineage, that by God's grace I have been blessed to make a mark upon the history of the human race, through my business and political contribution to Saint Lucia, my homeland.

Such a contribution could not have been possible without the magnanimous relationship I enjoyed with Mr. Leo Clarke and Prime Minister Dr. Kenny Anthony. Together, as a team, we ensured that Saint Lucia, this charming nation sitting with such glitter like a green jewel in the Caribbean Sea, would carry on after Sir John Compton's time was over—a stable, peaceful, harmonious, and free society making its mark as a twenty-first-century mecca for the world's vacationers.

Noel Cadasse
Ontario, Canada, 2013

part one

NOEL CADASSE: THE MAN AND HIS LIFE LESSONS

chapter one

THE RHYTHM OF THE LIFE

"Who will tell whether one happy moment of love, or the joy of breathing, or walking on a bright morning and smelling the fresh air, is not worth all the suffering and effort which life implies." —Erich Fromm

Life moves in ebbs and flows. Like the gentle rocking back and forth of the blue waves of the Caribbean Sea, life moves on the ocean of time with a rhythm; sometimes soft and gentle, sometimes harsh and hard. I have lived through both.

I saw this rhythm as a young boy; I understood it as a grown adult. I grew up playing on the ancient sandy shore of the Saint Lucian Caribbean Sea, washing my feet in the lapping waves, running into the receding water as a boy, rushing back to shore before the waves came back. I played with the ebb and flow of nature, wondering what lay beyond the distant horizon. As a young boy, my innocent eyes would gaze into the distance—that thin line where the blue sea meets the blue sky, where the elements embrace in glorious promise—and wonder what the future could be like. That distant horizon beckoned my young mind, calling me to a destiny and a fate that I would fifty years later discover to be the rhythm of human endurance and strength of character overcoming the weight of human weaknesses and failures.

I live today in Toronto, that quiet vibrant city in Canada where you can secure your life against the risks inherent in the constant ebb and flow of life. My life so far has shown me a harsh world. The world is not a place where the fulfillment of dreams comes easy to anyone. Life in this world is a daily fight, a battle against enormous odds. The system that makes up this world does not just hand out goodies to any human being. You are born into a world of struggle and pain and suffering. And you have to learn to dig your heels in and sweat it out and come out victorious—beaten and bruised, but victorious, the trophy of your dreams achieved clutched joyfully in your clenched hands.

Ebb and Flow

My life story—my losses and gains, my weaknesses and strengths, my failures and successes—inspires hope and faith. Dream big. Never give up. Be constant in one thing: believing in your dreams and hanging on to your destiny. Failure is just a temporary obstacle to direct you away from a wrong path into a new direction. Just believe that destiny is waiting for you ahead, and the obstacles along your life's path are signposts guiding you to reach the end of the journey in delightful triumph.

Life moves like the ebb and flow of the Caribbean Sea. In the distant horizon, for every human being, destiny and fate beckon; a challenge of life lived to the full, a fate of giving the human family a lasting legacy of good. Time. Time is the element that determines when we would leave the shifting sandy shore of our life and dare to venture out on the ebb and flow of the waves to reach for the distant, intimidating, brilliant blue horizon of our dreams. I dared. I lived. I reached out my grasping hand and dared to touch the horizon. I dared to live fully, allowing my latent human potential to overcome the enormous odds of my life, to touch the height of destiny and fate. Then I came back to tell the world what I learned. The life lesson of my story holds a wisdom and understanding that you will find inspiring, motivating and supremely beautiful.

chapter two

TO DREAM, TO CONQUER LIFE'S OBSTACLES

"The great use of life is to spend it for something that will outlast it."
—William James

Do you want to live your life to the full? Do you want to know the aesthetic joy of reaching for your dreams? Do you desire to grasp that beckoning star of your childhood dreams and hold it to your breast in delight, knowing that your power as a human being allows you to conquer any fear, any obstacle, any weakness? Life offers us so much. Yet so few dare to dream, to step out on the ebbing flow of the waves, and to reach out to their horizon. I have done it. And I am grateful for the lessons that I can now teach the young about life. I have had to find a depth of strength and courage, a reservoir of faith and hope, to overcome battling storms and raging obstacles and achieve a life history that stands tall among men who have graced this ancient earth.

I sit at my oak desk in a comfortable, soft chair in my business office in Toronto. Outside, the bright yellow sun shines down on a cold, snow-white city, sparkling and majestic on this biting winter day. The pure white snow on the ground reflects light into the air so that from inside the warm office, looking through the glass door, the day looks brilliant and inviting and welcoming. But stepping outside, the cold bites into your skin with chilling, bone-tingling reality.

I had driven through the crawling evening traffic—slow—on Toronto's wide highway to get to the office. I would be telling the world my life story. And here I sit on this chair intrigued, full of anticipation and expectation. As I sit behind that big polished brown oak desk in my purple leather chair, I wonder to myself—why would I even want to leave the Caribbean sun to spend the twilight of my years in the cold winter of Toronto, Canada? I want, through the writing of this book, to understand this. Why do people uproot themselves for "greener pastures"?

Ebb and Flow

My answer shocked me, left me sad and forlorn, nostalgic for my homeland. You see, I am a Caribbean Man. And as a Caribbean people, we have no roots. Moving from the Caribbean to Canada was not at all an uprooting. It was, rather, a moving on, a decision to shift geographic location. For the Caribbean people are drifters; their history starts at some indefinite time when they arrived on the islands from some mysterious, foreign place, and it includes them drifting on to England, the US, or Canada, among other distant lands. The present is a shifting uncertainty, like the sands on the shores of the Caribbean Sea, a constant ebb and flow, going out and coming in. To be solidly planted is a foreign idea in the mind of the Caribbean Man.

Oh, the Caribbean people do have a story. And this is my story. My story is a metaphor of the ebb and flow of the Caribbean islands, that fascinating place where daily life is a laid-back luxury for locals and tourists alike. It is a story wrapped up in the image of the shifting sands that make up the beautiful beaches, the people living their lives to mirror the shifting sands of time. Time, after all, determines our fate as human beings. Time to the Caribbean Man is like the shifting sand under his feet. My life story intrigues and excites this almost sociological excursion into the deeper consciousness of the Caribbean Man and his inner longings. And the probing question at the heart of the story is this: where did I come from and where am I going? Where did the Caribbean people come from, and where are they going? Where, in fact, do you as a human being come from, and where are you going? This is the essence of the Cadasse story, my story.

Someone said that life is not about the answers we come up with but about the questions we ask ourselves. My life story inspires us to ask the questions that would enhance our humanity, make us a more reflective people, and deepen our character and sensitivity to our world and the people who inhabit our life.

Today I walk the streets of winter-cold Toronto unknown, quiet, reserved from public life. Few people recognize my face. Yet I smile and remain a jovial man. This new life away from the spotlight of society finds me a humble man, a contented soul. But I know what the bright lights of public life can reveal in the depths of a man's character. I have tasted the dizzying fruits of success, of riding the waves of achievement, of dancing on the heights and summits of life's material progress.

chapter three

LIFE IN SAINT LUCIA

"Attitude is a little thing that makes a big difference." —Sir Winston Churchill

By the time I was thirty years old, I was a senior businessman in Saint Lucia. Later in life I entered public and community service, rising to the seat of a senator in the parliament's upper house. I sat there and pontificated to the nation in all my glory and pomp. The first time I got up to speak in parliament was a grand affair. There I was, my chest stuck out, my head held high, and the eloquent words flowing with such pride and self-importance. Oh, the little boy from Anse La Raye had grown up to conquer that big world out there.

I was born on December 24, 1945, in a poverty-stricken village in the backwoods of the tiny British colonial island called Saint Lucia in the Caribbean.

Saint Lucia sits like a paradise in the Caribbean Sea. From an airplane, the island emerges at first out of clouds like a speck of green dust in the big blueness of the sea. The national airport is small and cramped, like a small-town airport in Ontario. It is almost surprising to realize that this is where the plane would land to disembark passengers. As the plane descends to the airport, the island comes into focus as a mountainous landmass that looks like it's floating and could sink at any moment. As the plane makes its approach to land, the houses come into focus—houses perched precariously on the sides of mountains. The island is like a jewel in the blue sea, a small, valuable fertile land where green palm trees flourish, as a relief from the vast wideness of the blue sea merging with the blue sky.

It is also surprising that my country, this small space of a country, with a population of just 168,000 people, produced two Nobel Prize winners in the twentieth century—Derek Walcott, who won the Nobel Prize for Literature in 1992, and Sir William Arthur Lewis, who won the Nobel Prize for Economics in 1979.

Ebb and Flow

I came to know the aerial view of Saint Lucia only as an adult. As a boy I had only one view: in the vast shadow at the bottom of a mountain where our village perched with its flat, square one-room huts was the wide open sea with its ebbing and flowing blue waves. The huge mountain towered over us, covered in green forest and reaching to the clouds. I grew up with this idea of my own smallness and the bigness of the world—the sea stretching to merge with the distant horizon, and the mountain reaching up like the hand of God to disappear in clouds or on a clear day to merge with the blue sky.

In between the sea and the mountain, our village people dwell. Today the village is not much changed from how it was when I was born in 1945. Except for a few modern buildings and paved roads, the village remains the same, caught in a time warp, trapped in its simple village life.

It is a distinct testimony of the indomitable beauty of the human potential that I rose from my origins in this little backwater village to conquer the heights I have. I look back on my life with utmost humility and gratitude that I can sit here and write my life story. There are folks in Anse La Raye who have not been as fortunate as I have been in this life. Men and women older than I, or from the same generation as I, still walk the village the same as when they were children. But for me, the sea always beckoned towards the horizon. I felt small and alone in that world as a boy, but the landscape made such an impression on my young mind as I grew up that I have always lived with this restless longing, this yearning.

Growing up, I wanted to climb the mountain. I would look longingly at the people who had the means to conquer the face of that sturdy landscape to build mansions up there. I wanted to climb that mountain and stake my claim up there, not down here with the village people who worked on farms and caught and sold live fish for a living. I wanted to reach the horizon where the luxury cruise ships went, to be out there and up there, but not here. This restless reaching—for the horizon, for the top of the mountain—I have known not as clichés from books but in actual daily living. I have lived and experienced that reaching for the top of the mountain, the longing to conquer the sea and grasp the horizon.

As an island, Saint Lucia opened my eyes to perspectives, to views unavailable to people living in mainland countries. The landscape of the country was shaped by the sea. The sea defines the country, dictating not only the physical shape and geography, but the worldview and life outlook of the people who inhabit the island. I can see why people in villages like Anse La Raye would feel trapped and helpless, would almost give up on striving. The sea is so big and vast and wide and endless that it seems to be the master that keeps the people in its borders. Venturing out to the sea was not an option. You stayed close to shore or faced death. Indeed, I have experienced the death by drowning of a brother because he stepped out too far into the sea.

And looking the other way did not bring much relief: the mountain towers above everything and everyone. High above us, way up in the sky, the mountain rises and rises and rises, endless into the clouds and the blue sky. In between this enormous mountain and vast sea, the people live in square one-room huts; a people rugged and close to the land. When I grew up there, most spent their days bent over in the hot sun planting the fertile ground with cassava and eddoe roots or banana, sugar cane, or vegetables; others spent their days in rough open boats in the sea catching fish for sale in the local market. The market brought the village together, a hard, rough people, speaking the French Creole language despite over a century of British rule, the language having a hard accent to it that reflects the hardness of life lived close to the ground, off the land and the sea.

chapter four

THE EMIGRANT LONGING

"Civilization is the limitless multiplication of unnecessary necessities."
—Mark Twain

Our family did not take to the land or the sea. We sought to escape this fate. My older brother emigrated to England as soon as he was old enough to travel on his own, and after my father died, we abandoned farming. My mother took to baking, and I assumed the role of village baker. This soft occupation prepared me for a life off the land. I became a baker, and our family today owns the premier bakery business in the country.

But the land and the sea have forever stamped my worldview with that restless longing to conquer ever greater heights. My life has been this journey of conquest, this restless longing to conquer the impossible. And in the process I have discovered that there is a rhythm to life, like the ebb and flow of the Caribbean Sea. The mountain always stands steady and sturdy, immovable and unmovable, while the sea shifts with its constant ebb and flow. In between these two, I grew up to learn one thing: the journey of life is an ebb and flow, a steady rhythm, a dancing through the tiny space between the mountain of achievements and the sea of misfortunes.

On the one hand, there is the wide-open fluidity of the sea, the chance to embark upon the waves and reach out to touch the horizon. On the other hand is the solid stability of the mountain. I ventured out on the sea, I reached for the horizon; I lived a full and adventurous life, denying myself very little that my heart desired. And on that journey, many times in my zeal to reach the horizon, I sank or got blown off track or just toppled over, under the weight of my own ambition and eager reaching. And always, I could turn back to the stability of that mountain and know that at its stable foot is my home, my little village, where I can always go back and find the warmth and care of loving people. In

Ebb and Flow

life, reach for your dreams and strive to achieve your best, but remember to stake a stable cord where your tent can find a permanent place, where you can go back and stand on solid ground, safe in the care and comfort of the mountain.

In my life's journey of adventure, where I surf the ebb and flow of life, I have constantly had to turn to the stability of my wife, Julia. She has been a tower of strength in my life. She has been to me like that mountain that shadowed our village and stood as a solid rock for me as a boy. No matter how far I wandered, the mountain was always there, visible from anywhere on the island or anywhere on the sea around Saint Lucia. While I surf the sea of life, my wife has been the solid, stable force that has built a fortress on the mountain of life, and she graciously welcomes me every time I suffer a setback on my journey.

Over the course of this journey, I became a household name in Saint Lucia. I achieved high office and glorious riches. But it was Julia, this woman who worked as a teacher while raising five children, who provided the foundation for this life journey. We were married when I was twenty-two years old, when I was a member of the Royal Saint Lucia Police Force, and today, in our sixties, she continues to be the solid mountain of strength in my life.

It is because of Julia that I became a household name in Saint Lucia. It is because of her that I could make the contributions that I made in our community, in service to our country for thirty solid years. She caused me to venture where I would have been too frightened to venture, were she not with me.

Although it was easy entering the world of business as far back as forty years ago when I first joined the First Federation Life Insurance Company, she stood by me, always encouraging me on. I moved on to form the first locally owned life insurance company in Saint Lucia, the First National Insurance Company. Back then it was not easy because to start up any business, you need capital and you need expertise. The two go hand in hand. Capital was a major problem, not only for myself, but for many people who aspired to start small businesses in the country. To acquire capital to start a business and to get it going before it can start earning is quite difficult, even now. So I have suffered extreme difficulty venturing into the business world in my homeland—that Caribbean paradise named Saint Lucia. A small island nation is not the ideal place to achieve great things: great achievement is beyond the horizon, away from the land. This lesson was a hard one for me to learn.

chapter five

PERSPECTIVE OF SUCCESS

"You must be the change you wish to see in the world." —Mahatma Gandhi

I believe that my whole life has been successful. I measure success not by what you achieve from an economic viewpoint, because I don't think there is very much from an economic point to talk about. I have always based success on what you have achieved for people in the community—what you've achieved in shaping the lives of people, in helping them to excel in life. And this is where I like to see my success. I have helped to shape the lives of many, many people. I have seen people grow because of my influence in their lives. I have seen people who I reached out to benefit and live a more fulfilling life. So that's the kind of success I like to talk about—what I have done for others and what those people have achieved by virtue of my contribution to their well-being.

Today I live my belief as a Pentecostal Christian man. But even before I decided to turn my heart to live as a disciple of the Lord Jesus Christ, leaders in Saint Lucia were recognizing the depths of my core character strength. My fellow Saint Lucian, broadcaster and journalist Willie James, wrote a glowing tribute to my love for the compassionate life of kindness. This is not to say that I am a saint—far from it. But I believe in community. I believe that to achieve my dreams, I had to become a people person. I had to love people and live with a kind and compassionate heart. I believe that it is out of giving of yourself that you acquire greatness. Greatness is thrust upon people by others. So in reaching out to others and helping as much as I could to make life easier and more bearable for them, I have been given back wealth, power, and a comfortable life. I am eternally grateful for this blessing.

Even in opening an insurance company, I recognized that basic social services were lacking in the country—health care especially. I opened an insurance company to provide insurance for people to be able to improve their quality of life. Out of this service-oriented life, some people came to recognize my contributions. This is what journalist Willie James said in 2001:

"When we peer into the mystery that is our life, we would see that life is, in essence, a complex celebration of many wonders. Each of us performs our own significant role in this mystery. We proceed to become familiar with that special role we perform on the theatre stage of life. The casting, however, may not be up to us. The producer and director—our Creator God—commands that centre stage. And on that stage, one of life's distinguished actors, within the Saint Lucia context, has been Cadasse.

"Born on Christmas Eve in 1945, I find it interesting that Cadasse shares the birthday of Jesus Christ, the greatest man who ever graced the earth. Born in the tiny village of Anse La Raye on the edge of the wide blue Caribbean Sea, he began his stage role as the twelfth of fourteen children, born to poor parents, Eudoxia and George Cadasse. His parents faced enormous struggle to house and feed and nurture so many children.

"This struggle impacted Cadasse's young mind. He absorbed all the thrills and pains of this hard start to life, learning the lessons that would prepare him for his role in life. He grew in strength and learned the hard lessons that would allow him to become a full-blooded capitalist businessman, cementing his place in the competitive market place. The sibling rivalry helped him develop fighting muscles for the business world.

"In these early days of his life preparation, Cadasse struggled. But those years taught him the fighting spirit, the fundamental principles of achieving personal growth and development despite the battles in his way. These principles of dogged determination shaped his psyche, moulding his ability to respond to adversity and pain with resolve and strength.

"Cadasse never gives up in life. He plays his role with the spirit of a determined fighter, getting up and going again every time he gets knocked down. He learned early that to achieve anything of value and worth, he had to do the little things right. The little things add up to the big achievement. Whether at play, work, home doing the chores, school, in his relationships, love, or business, Cadasse perseveres, never

Perspective of Success

giving up on his dreams. His struggles saw him never getting a college education, but he excels as a student of life.

"This mystery of life that he was born to face and conquer sketched for him a script rooted in the struggle-escape rhythm. His one driving force has been his desire to live a successful life. His early training and discipline in the Royal Saint Lucia Police Force paved the way for him to blaze new trails in the Caribbean business jungle. Early on, Cadasse embraced his role in life with positive zeal, recognizing the glowing unlimited prospects for him as a man. He struggled hard, and learned to perfect his role into an art form, living his life with such outstanding humility and peaceful content that his children have come to admire his ability to absorb the pressures of his constant striving upward. Restless ambition pushes him forward. His ambition makes him see open opportunities that he grasps with deft hands, believing in his ability and his inner strength. Many of those opportunities collapsed under his hands, and failure threatened to dampen his enthusiasm for his life role. But each time he would rise up again, his damp spirit ablaze with new zeal. He might be knocked down, but he gets up to fight another day. He has owned national businesses—hotels, restaurants, bakeries, insurance companies. He knows the terrain of this life. He navigates his way forward and upward, pushing each obstacle out of his way, his eyes fixed on the top of his mountain—success as a human being in his society. Cadasse worked with zeal and strength, contributing so much to Saint Lucia's development as a new nation. He plays his role on life's stage with compassion, skill and class."

chapter six

THE PATH OF PEACE

"Be great in act, as you have been in thought." —William Shakespeare

I rose to the top of my world in Saint Lucia, riding the waves of success with great pomp and pride. Then one day, my dream world collapsed around me. After twenty-five years riding a high wave as businessman, politician, and sought-after socialite in my homeland, I saw my world plunge beneath the waves of misfortune that bedevils most self-made men.

In moments of collapse, life reveals so much to the sensitive heart. Material success can so easily mask the real stuff of life. For me, the world was a perfect place of material success. I had it all. I had achieved such outstanding success that multitudes of friends gathered around me, sponging off my goodwill and my heart of love for people. But for anyone basking in the wonders of the spotlight, dancing on the stage of success, darkness will one day overwhelm. And when that darkness hit me, I stood stunned and transfixed, for no one stood with me. For the first time in my life, when I most needed friends and business partners to prop me up, to hold my head above the rising waves of failures—in this moment of drowning under the weight of my own ambition and pride, I stood alone. It scared me. I stared with disbelief as friend after friend abandoned me and turned against me with indifference and contempt.

In this time, my moment of crisis, I did not even feel like I could turn to the Catholic church where I had spent my whole life. This was because I had conflicted with the church's doctrine over my support in parliament for Saint Lucia's tourism development. Now I had no faith that I would find solace there. I just did not feel that the priests or anyone in the church could help. The darkness was everywhere. I could not see any light anywhere. I felt alone, lost, abandoned, beaten, and broken. It was a terrifying nightmare.

Ebb and Flow

Now I recall the memories of those days from my posh, cool business office in Canada, as winter showers the parking lot with cold icy snow. Yet in that dark world of dread, divine help showed a merciful face. Someone told me that if I turned to a Pentecostal church close to my home, I might find some sympathetic ear. I was desperate. Times were desperate, and, as the proverbial drowning man, I reached out for any straw that promised some kind of hope. So I bit my pride back and walked into a Pentecostal church, the Bethel Tabernacle, for the first time in my life. That day changed my life forever.

My wife, Julia—the amazing woman who stood by me all this time, that stable force who has been the mountain of strength in my life and who never gave up on me—and I decided to go to this church and ask the pastor to intercede with God for us. I was always a deeply religious man, and so the idea to approach God was natural to me. However, to turn away from the Catholic church and seek out the intercession of a Pentecostal pastor was quite revolutionary for my family. We went to a pastor at this Pentecostal church, and to our amazement, he came to our house to pray with us after our first visit to his church. He started a regular Saturday visit to us after that, praying with us through this whole ordeal. God was reaching out to us in our darkest moment.

In my heart I felt that all this was happening for a purpose. In my success and my prideful living, I had forgotten the idea of humility to turn to God. But like Job and so many men whom God touched, I had to face the darkness. The terrifying truth of this world system had to knock me hard in the face for me to wake up and see the light of God's mercy. Now I am so much more humble and merciful and kind. I have known the favour of God. And today, I am a better man for it, a man of deeper character, of greater depth in my spirit.

I do not know what I would have done without that pastor's kindness. I did contemplate suicide at one point. It was so difficult to lose everything I had worked so hard for. And to face society as everything around me collapsed—it was too much. At those moments in life, it was as if life became unbearable. Nothing mattered to me. I faced inner demons, tormented with terrible thoughts of failure and humiliation. I walked with my eyes turned inwards, looking for something inside me to hold on to, some inner strength. Yet all I found was fear and terror, frightened of failure.

My fall surprised me. I had rose through the ranks of business—from an insurance salesman to assistant manager within nine months, then general manager in just two years. I used to be a rising star. Within five years, I had bought the company I worked for, becoming my country's first owner of a life insurance

The Path of Peace

company. I aptly named the firm the First National Insurance Company, as it was the first such business locally owned in Saint Lucia.

I had come from a poor little village, and there I was, still in my early twenties, owning Saint Lucia's first insurance company. After moving away from the village to live in the city, I never looked back. In fact, there was nothing to look back to. I had escaped the little world of Anse La Raye, my boyhood village where I had played on the shores of the vast Caribbean Sea, wondering what lay beyond the distant blue horizon. And by the age of twenty-two years, I had escaped my world of poverty.

chapter seven

THE POLITICAL ALLURE

"History will be kind to me, for I intend to write it." —Sir Winston Churchill

Those early years of business were exciting times. My company excelled. My life evolved into a great experience. I achieved so much. When Saint Lucia gained political independence from Britain in 1979 under the leadership of Sir John Compton, I was excited for the new future. Saint Lucians could finally control and channel their own destiny. And here I was well-positioned to lead in the financial sector. Politics had delivered our nation. We had moved out of the shadow of the mighty British Empire to chart our own course, to ourselves conquer the distant horizon. The nation celebrated the politician who did it, Sir John Compton, who had shifted the big mountain of the empire and opened the way to the future for us.

And so to politics I turned. If politics had become the saviour of the people, able to wrench social and economic power away from the British colonial masters, then politics must be the panacea for me to stamp my vision of Saint Lucia on the new country's consciousness.

Eighteen years after Saint Lucia's independence from Britain, I joined the Saint Lucia Labour Party, determined to contribute to the development of my homeland. I had grown up from that young boy from Anse La Raye to become a social and economic leader in my country. And I decided how to reach my horizon and how to take my little village, along with my country, into the future as I envisioned it.

I had seen the power of politics after Compton conquered the British Empire. So after I suffered a public humiliation at the malicious hand of a government minister, I joined the Saint Lucia Labour Party. The prime minister at the time, Dr. Vaughn Lewis, had demanded a public apology on national television from me to him, because I had made negative comments in the media about his leadership of the country. At the time, I was the president of the Saint Lucia Hotel and Tourism Association. I suffered the public humiliation of having to apologize publicly to the prime minister. And I decided that I would join the opposition, the Saint Lucia Labour Party, and help it get into power, to defeat Lewis.

The Labour Party won the next elections, ending the more than twenty-year reign of Lewis's party. Politics had delivered my victory. I had become acting chairman of the Labour Party and led it to victory in 1997. (My inaugural victory speech to the party is published in Part Two of this book.) Life is an ebb and flow: out of the humiliation, here I was, a man of enormous political and economic power.

However, becoming a politician may have been my biggest mistake on my life's journey. After gaining political power, I got over the petty rivalry with Lewis and became excited for the role I could now play. I thought that politics would answer all the problems facing the young nation.

In the squalor and poverty of Anse La Raye when I was growing up, I had seen my mother suffer terribly because she was a poor single mother. My mother was of French descent. She was a quiet, proud woman. She operated the village's bakery, waking up at 4:00 a.m. to bake bread on a brick stove with old wood for fuel. She did this to raise her children after my father died in our early childhood. I thought that I could erase this poverty that had afflicted me as a child and that had seen my mother face so much tragedy—through the social power of politics. That was a big mistake, really bad judgment on my part.

I jumped into the political arena, and the game chewed me up. I spent money wildly, throwing it at every possible avenue to garner votes and political community support. I have witnessed the deceit of the politician—only votes matter. This attitude of the average politician in the Caribbean has not changed, even today. Many of them are still in the "horse and carriage" days—stuck in petty power struggles and party infighting, only interested in votes to stay in power. I have lost faith in some of the political leaders in my own country. That is one reason why I emigrated to Canada.

My life journey—my successes, strivings, dreams, and failures—is a metaphor of the Caribbean people today. My life is a microcosm of the larger picture that makes up the Caribbean region. The Caribbean people strive and achieve. But they lose and suffer failure, because the political system holds the nation back, with many leaders caught in a stupor in the headlight of power, pomp, and pride. Sudden power handed to ordinary people in a new nation

The Political Allure

becomes a recipe for even more suffering for the people than under the heavy, weighty hand of colonial hard-heartedness.

After Saint Lucia became independent of British rule in 1979, there was no social safety net for the people. My insurance company came in and provided that safety net. People could suddenly be insured against the damaging forces of nature. We were providing vital services to the people. Private entrepreneurship filled a key gap in the nation's social system. We provided life insurance for the first time to people all over, including Anse La Raye, with the intention that their quality of life would increase as people gained access to expensive health care.

But the power of the political system, after the bright light that it had ignited in the people's heart for gaining them total independence from the British Empire—this power rooted in the perception of the masses—pulled me into its grip. People thought politicians could do anything, that they were more powerful than anyone or anything. But if the governments of the Caribbean were not so selfish, the region could become such a glorious haven for its people. I have seen this up close and personal. The Caribbean right now has enough people of talent and resources and skill and education and experience, living overseas in the US, Canada, Britain, and elsewhere, who can contribute so much to its development—economic, social, and political. But many of the local politicians erect sturdy walls cemented on their greed and selfishness. They want no one to come in on what they see as their territory. They shut out those who could do more than they could. They suffer from a severe inferiority complex. They therefore fuel terrible misfortunes, unnecessary obstacles, and crucial setbacks as the people strive to achieve their dreams.

How many of my own friends and neighbours could not escape from the foothill of the mountain at Anse La Raye and venture out to their horizon because of this political quagmire? I can only wonder in sadness.

chapter eight

REACHING FOR A DREAM

"A vote is like a rifle: its usefulness depends on the character of the user."
—Theodore Roosevelt

I had seen the writing on the wall for nations like Saint Lucia. Achieving your dreams could not be done without venturing out across the vastness of the sea into a new world, a bigger world. Since 1981, I had sensibly secured my Canadian citizenship. But I never had an interest in living in Canada—or anywhere other than my native Saint Lucia—permanently. I wanted to see my nation grow and develop. I was born there. I grew up there. I wanted to see that independence from Britain would give us as a people the chance to rise in status in the world. I wanted to play my part, to bring my people forward and see them achieve outstanding success as a nation. All I wanted to do was play my part in the nation's development process, to see Anse La Raye rise to the top of the mountain and venture out from the edge of the sea to conquer the horizon.

Yet in 2002, in the twilight of my years, after living in Saint Lucia for fifty years, I had to emigrate with my family. The Caribbean leaders are not seeing the bigger picture of life. The politicians seem only to want to remain in power. They do not foster the national cohesion that is necessary for the development of a nation. There must be greater relationship building for the Caribbean Man. We have not yet learned how to build relationships that are lasting and that can ride the waves of life's fortunes and misfortunes. It's a mindset thing. Even the region's world-class cricket team is suffering from this mental fragility, this myopic worldview, where they are too small and the landscape too big.

After independence, I was very excited about the Caribbean. The 1960s were such promising times. We thought if the British handed over our destiny and our moulding totally to us, we could make our future; we could dream big and aim high, scale the mountain and conquer the sea. Well, I tried. I aimed high. I dreamed. I reached for the horizon. And what do I have to show for it today? Unfortunately I felt that I was forced out of Saint Lucia, out of the Caribbean development process. Here I am in Toronto, Canada, contributing to the business climate of this city. Why? Why can we in the Caribbean not hold hands with each other and help each other take the nation to greater heights? Why are the politicians so heady and high with the sudden power handed to them? Where are our visionaries and our leaders of integrity? These are serious questions we must all start asking.

Back then I was so excited about our future. Now I am very worried about the Caribbean. The Caribbean today sits like an idyllic paradise on the majestic blue sea, a haven for tourists from all over the world. The region boasts the best places of relaxation anywhere on the planet. Yet the local people all have eyes to emigrate north to the US or Canada. Everybody wants to emigrate. Little is being done to encourage people to seek opportunities within the Caribbean. Few leaders speak of the opportunities that people can grasp in their homeland. It is very difficult to find a way to work with the powers that be.

If I were the prime minister of Saint Lucia, I would educate the young people on the knowledge of the country's economy. There is too much of a dependency syndrome in the Caribbean. The young people need to be educated as to the local opportunities that are available to them. When I started my insurance business back in the 1970s, I saw the opportunities that were open to me to help the local population live fulfilling lives. I saw the need for the social services I could offer through insurance. And my company served a great need in society.

Today, people are not looking for what they can do for the nation. All they want is to emigrate to the bright lights of some big city in North America. And the politicians are taken up with their grasping for power. This leaves the young people in a bad situation. Young people become very complacent. In the Caribbean today, young people know about the materialistic life North America offers them. And this is all they aspire to. They have so much knowledge of the world. When I was a young person, I was so innocent of the ways of the world. I strived only to do my best for society, to contribute my best to my country. But knowledge can be a dangerous thing. The knowledge of the material way of life that young people can have today has robbed them of the innocence that would see them become good citizens of their own country. My childhood of hard work, discipline, simplicity, and innocence shaped my life and achievements.

The leaders of the Caribbean today are failing to show the children and the young people the value of hard work. We have to shift the mental paradigm of

Reaching for a Dream

the people to give greater value to the latent human potential of their lives. They need mentors, solid local role models, and a safety net that would cushion them when life's misfortunes strike.

I learned one important life lesson from my experiences, especially in the time of crisis that saw me emigrate from the stultifying environment of the Caribbean to the more stable Canada.

chapter nine

SOCIETY NEEDS SAFETY NETS

"Judge a man by his questions rather than his answers." —Voltaire

I learned that everyone needs a system that you can turn to for comfort and solid advice in times of crisis or doubt. Everyone needs to know that there is a mountain standing tall and majestic and solid and anchored, there forever, stable and ready to provide a safe haven.

We are humans, with human faults and frailties. And when we fall, our society should have in place people who are selfless and wise and knowledgeable, who can lead us back to the right path, who are strong and stable and solid.

I could not find this in Saint Lucia. When I fell, after twenty-five years in business, the one who helped me find hope was a pastor. But he could not help put my business back together. I found my spiritual salvation through his prayers with my family and his counselling. But I lost all faith in my country. I could not find the strength to believe that I could build a solid economic or socially satisfying life in Saint Lucia anymore. I had ventured out on life's journey, riding the waves and the ebbs and flows. But when I turned to the Saint Lucian political system, I found that they had abandoned the mountain for the glitz and glamour of political power, leaving the new nation to sink as it was learning to swim.

I sought to give as much as I could to Saint Lucia. After scaling the summit of my dreams—touching the beauty of the horizon—in my business achievements, I leapt into the political arena convinced that I could play a part to shape Saint Lucia for the good of all the people.

It was not to be.

Business and politics do not go hand in hand in the Caribbean. As a businessperson, I was supposed to be silent, out of the public spotlight. The chances of achieving noble visions for the country as a politician are not good. There is too much in-fighting within political parties, too much jealous rage among power seekers, too much petty insecurity among the political elite. In fact, my experience in the Caribbean has taught me that small societies are prone to this sort of problem, where political elites can easily play the power game for personal "handouts."

The whole system functions like that. Saint Lucia depends on handouts from the developed world. The country still has blackouts. It still has places where there is no running water. This comes from a complacent attitude. Most people are so complacent, concerned primarily with what they can get from the system. The nation has lost the sound social values of our Judeo-Christian heritage in my generation. This generation caters to material greed. The nation goes to church on Sundays, but if Christianity is going to church on Sunday without living a transformed life, then what's the point? I have not seen Saint Lucia transformed so every citizen could achieve their dream.

I have lost confidence in the political and socio-economic system that has choked the country into a place of development stagnation. Even as a Catholic I had lost confidence in the type of Christianity I was practicing—the moral and ethical structure of the society. The moral and ethical foundation was there, but I was just going to church, going through the motions. The commitment to the realities of a truly spiritual life, I just did not have.

In fact, I was against what the Catholic church stood for, even when I was an altar boy, because the priest slapped and beat me. The church has failed to be the moral bedrock of the society. So when I needed some spiritual guidance, I could not turn to the place where I had worshipped all my life.

In 1999, I became a "born-again" Christian, because the pastor from the Pentecostal church showed me the realities of Christian living. Even in my darkest, most bitter moment of my life, he came in as a stranger and stood with me, prayed with me, and helped me find hope and meaning and purpose. But it had to take a monumental collapse of my life for me to find him. I had woken up one day and found I had lost everything I had worked for all my life. I couldn't even buy food. Nobody was there for me. My best of friends, family, the politicians I had helped elect to power—all turned their backs on me.

But Pastor Emmanuel McLaurens came to my house with some people from the church and ministered to me. I can remember vividly having a strong urge to commit suicide. But he was there, ministering to me every week—bringing to me the peace that only the Lord Jesus Christ can impart to a suffering soul. I joined a men's prayer group. I gained new friends in the church and turned to this life of faith. For more than a year, that's all I did.

chapter ten

THE FALL AND FORGIVENESS

"It is easier to forgive an enemy than to forgive a friend." —William Blake

You never really see it coming when you are falling—it just happens. And when it happened to me, I became a very bitter person until I accepted the forgiveness and love of the Lord. Then I knew that my whole life was shaped and moulded for His glory. I realized that every incident in my life was a preparation. My real fundamental life lesson is this—that there is a real God and He is alive and He cares. Today, I am much more humble and subdued. My life is directed by a spiritual awareness. I pray every day. In fact, I always have my Bible laying on my desk at my office.

I have learned to be more charitable to people, to be more forgiving, less aggressive. I place God first in my life. I do more to have a more honest relationship with my family. And I would never go into politics again. I have learned not to spend my days organizing social functions and so on, but to make my time more beneficial and spend more time with my family.

Stay close to family. Stay close to God. In times of trouble, in the ebb and flow of this life's journey, only faith in God guides you to the path of peaceful, joyous living. I once thought power as a politician would do it for me. I have learned that faith in the Lord Jesus Christ is the best guarantor for the ebbs and flows of life's great journey.

To conquer the sea and reach the horizon, to build a mansion on the mountain top, to bring social and economic development to Anse La Raye, I needed to reach the place where I put my faith and trust in the One who designs our journey for us.

Through all the travails and triumphs of my life, I have come to the summit of understanding that the way to achieve my potential as a human being is faith in my Creator. He created me and designed me, and therefore He knows

Ebb and Flow

best how to take me to where my heart desires. In a life of ebbs and flows, of uncertainty, unpredictable occurrences, where misfortune and achievement interchange so readily, what better mountain to hold on to than faith in the One who is omnipotent?

chapter eleven

THE DREAM OF THE MAN

"To accomplish great things, we must dream as well as act." —Anatole France

My business place is an elite banquet hall that sits majestic amid the sprawling red brick warehouses that make up the industrial neighbourhood of the city of Woodbridge, just north of the Toronto metropolitan economic hub.

Surrounding the building where I work every day, several elite service companies make the vibrant area home—like the luxury limousine company, with elegant sparkling limousines dotting the parking lot. This shopping plaza attracts the well-to-do, the people with big money to spend on lavish ceremonies—weddings, parties, receptions, business meetings, gala shows, and upscale refined gatherings.

Every morning I walk across the dark marble-tiled floor in the waiting area into my spacious office to manage the affairs of the elite service establishment. The ceiling is high and dotted with powerful little lights. The place exudes an atmosphere of luxury.

I grew up in Saint Lucia wondering what the world held for me. As a boy, the endless Caribbean Sea beckoned my young mind to reach for the horizon. In my heart, I developed a Caribbean Dream. I wanted to achieve outstanding success with my life. My life has been a reaching out in this quest to conquer.

As a boy growing up in a family afflicted at every turn under the oppressive hand of poverty, I determined early that I would demand my fair due from the world. Today, my constant, restless quest to achieve my Caribbean Dream has taken me to the management seat of the banquet and entertainment centre, and in the process, I am changing the entertainment scene in Toronto, Ontario.

Everyone recognizes that Canada's most metropolitan cities are going through dynamic demographic shifts. More and more ethnic communities are gaining significant socio-economic power. I ride this wave at the very top, enjoying surfing the Toronto business world. When I found out that the banquet hall was up for sale, I was relatively new to Canada, having immigrated to Toronto less than five years earlier. After a couple years struggling to get a footing in the city—trying my hand at door-to-door sales, a management job at another banquet hall, and network marketing—I decided to do what I do best. I launched out with full and absolute confidence to capture a new vision for my life from the distant horizon.

Ignoring my short time in Canada as an immigrant, I approached several financial institutions—based solely on my thirty years of experience in the hospitality and business arena—in the sprawling bustling rich city of Toronto, Ontario, with a daring proposal. I was determined to operate my own hospitality business in Canada.

I had met an accomplished businessman at a networking marketing event. And when two entrepreneurial minds collide, sparks are bound to ignite into full-fledged economic opportunity. I had helped this person gain a solid foothold in the economy of Saint Lucia—including setting up an indigenous bank and an insurance company.

Now I decided to pitch to this financial guru the idea for the Caribbean community to own one of Toronto's most elite service establishments. This person not only bought the idea of backing me in the deal but agreed to buy equity in the business. We aimed to transform the landscape of the entertainment sector, bringing to Canada the first luxury Caribbean-community-owned banquet hall and convention centre.

The deal illustrates how I have learned to live my life. I dream big, jump high, and seek to conquer huge obstacles. My life is a roller-coaster ride, as I live with the burning quest to achieve my Caribbean Dream.

That Caribbean Dream quest had left me shattered and lost by the end of the last century. The year 2000 saw me a broken man. After twenty-five years in business in Saint Lucia, as an icon in the country, achieving the status of becoming a "household name"; after amassing $30 million in business ventures; after rising to the rank of senator in the Saint Lucian government; after leading the Saint Lucia Labour Party to a walloping election victory as acting chairman of the party; after raising my family of five children with my wife, Julia; after pioneering several businesses across Saint Lucia—after achieving my Caribbean Dream and rising to stardom as a self-made Caribbean Man, I saw it all collapse in one moment of dreadful agony.

The Dream of the Man

I remember the day, clear as the sunny blue sky that lights up the rocking waves of the Caribbean Sea. The day the police came to escort me and my eldest son from our offices at the famous Caribbees Hotel on the island state. I had built the hotel from nothing. It had made my life and joy. And here the police were, escorting me out of the doors into the street with my son in tow. That moment of humility stripped me bare before the world. My Caribbean Dream had collapsed. Spectacular and sudden, I lost everything I had worked for all my life. My family and I would never be the same again. I felt betrayed that this place that had hosted so much government and party business, to a great extent on a complimentary basis, would be allowed by the same government to collapse.

The Caribbees is a majestic, palatial hotel built into the top of a mountain overlooking the Caribbean Sea. It offers a spectacular panoramic view of Saint Lucia's lush, green palm trees and inviting blue beaches. The hotel is an oasis of luxury, with its rooftop patio, mountain-top swimming pool, and breathtaking window views from the rooms.

The drive into the hotel follows a narrow winding road climbing the mountain at a forty-five-degree angle. The approach is amazing, and inside the gates, the hotel becomes a serene place of relaxation and rest. I loved the place, the atmosphere. To have this as a business was such a joy to me.

But the business had gone into receivership because I was then taken up with the political office that I had secured through the Saint Lucia Labour Party. As senator and chairman of the gaming commission, I concentrated my efforts in public service and neglected my private business ventures. The result was that I lost the businesses through the bank's receivership. This experience caused me to eventually migrate from Saint Lucia, which was a painful decision for me to make.

Yet I reinvented myself. I got up, dusted myself off, washed my feet of the Caribbean sand, boarded a plane, and headed for Toronto, Canada. I was going to use this failure to rise higher, to expand my Caribbean Dream on the international stage. *I will win,* I thought, as my wife and I quietly left our homeland behind for the cold white winter of Canada.

My days now at the banquet hall are filled with laughter, contentment, and peace. Canada has delivered to me and my family the blessing of accomplishment, of achievement. And what the Caribbean lost in my human resources potential, Canada has gained in value. My management style at the banquet hall is to lead by the golden rule—"Do unto others as you would like them do unto you." And I am assured that with this principle in operation, the business is sure to prosper.

Ebb and Flow

Why did a brilliant entrepreneur fail to achieve his Caribbean Dream in the Caribbean? Why did I have to come to North America to contribute my talents and receive my right rewards? What is it about the Caribbean that its brightest and best are shoved out and they ship to "greener pastures"?

And then, why is it that once they ship out of the blue sea, they never forget their Caribbean-ness? When I gave the keynote address at the gala opening of a previous banquet hall business under my ownership, the elegant guests heard me extol the virtues of the Caribbean community owning their own luxury banquet hall and convention centre. I stressed the beauty of people of the Caribbean coming together to make the business a shining reality. Yet those brilliant Caribbean sons and daughters—who achieve such astonishing success in Canada—had left the Caribbean broken, disillusioned, and filled with bitterness for their homeland. Why could they not do this in their homeland?

The question triggers me to launch into a lecture about the shortcomings of the political leadership class in the Caribbean. Many of the politicians mess things up for the people, and the thought of how much I have suffered at the hands of petty politics makes me red in the face with pent-up anger and frustration. Clearly, I would much prefer to live and build in my native land. But I am realistic enough to understand when a socio-economic environment is not conducive to my entrepreneurial mentality.

Ironic and sad it is that I have to realize my Caribbean Dream in Canada. The Caribbean today pushes in its effort to unite the nations that sprawl across the Caribbean Sea into a united economic zone, à la Europe. And I find great delight in pointing out that I bring this unity of Caribbean-ness—a one-people, one-nation mentality—to work in the entertainment business.

This is what the Caribbean needs more than ever—for resourceful people to network and partner for the growth and development of the region's economy. Why do we have to come to North America to do this?

chapter twelve

BIRTHDAY REFLECTIONS

"We need men who can dream of things that never were." —John F. Kennedy

I celebrated my sixtieth birthday on Christmas Eve in 2006. I held a lavish little party in Toronto for special invitees to celebrate the Christmas season and toast my birthday. My family and friends stood as one to toast the man of the hour, smiling and happy. I had made it again in life. The year was ending on a high note for me. But few of the guests could sense the emotions gripping my stomach: the rhythm of life had seen me come to this point a thoroughly humbled man.

As I stood to acknowledge the round of applause that went up for my birthday toast, my mind saw a flashback of my hotel, the fifty-six-room Caribbees with its 1,000-capacity conference centre. After the hotel went into receivership, a Guyanese outfit called Cara Suites bought it and ran it within a couple years back into receivership. That collapsed dream had shattered my faith in the Caribbean environment ever being able to deliver the dream of its nationals—people born into the land but forced to move on as ever-drifting migrants.

When I came to Canada, however, that desire for achieving above the ordinary, to make the most of my life, pushed me to continue my quest, to expand my dream. It was this desire that led me to believe that I could build back my business life in Canada.

My Jamaican-born business partner and I put our resources together and bought this 40,000-square-foot entertainment centre. Within a few short years, I had propelled myself to become a leader in the Canadian Caribbean business community. The banquet hall presents a fantastic opportunity for me to use my skills on a more international stage. I always had a passion for the hospitality industry. It is something I love to do. Apart from owning the Caribbees, I also served Saint Lucia as head of the Saint Lucia Hotel and Tourism Association, and as director of the Saint Lucia Tourist Board. I was bringing this skill, experience, and full training to the Toronto hospitality industry.

I want to make this business into a totally multicultural centre. The 40,000-square-foot space and 1,000-capacity convention hall could be used to promote the multicultural idea that is so much a part of what Canada is but also so much of what the Caribbean is all about.

How could I have such a vision? I grew up poor in Saint Lucia. Poverty really impacted me. My mom and dad had seventeen children in all. Five died very early in childhood. My father died when I was fourteen. He fell sick and died. I grew up in a tiny square hut on a muddy pathway that served as a street in Anse La Raye, a cramped village on the edge of the Caribbean Sea. In this space, my mother raised twelve children.

The village is perched at the bottom of a great massive mountain that looms over it. Sandwiched between this mountain and the vastness of the sea, I grew up feeling trapped in a small space. I decided early in life that I would escape these confines; that I would go beyond the mountain and over the sea.

In business and then in politics, I sought to escape, to conquer the towering bigness of the world around me. The hard, grinding poverty that I knew as a child still haunts the village. People there live hard and rugged and with a resignation to their fate that is depressing to witness. Their faces become lined and wrinkled early in life. Yet they remain a jovial people, with laughter filling the air.

The new generation also has that sense of abandonment as my generation did, but now they have TV and the new ideas that come from travellers and from those who have educated themselves and seen a bigger picture of life. The young are starting to move out quickly.

The village has a lot of older folks. But in my days there, life was an experience that I did not cherish, despite the innocence I can now remember with fondness. What strikes me about the village and childhood is the innocence, the lack of resentment at how hard things were or how small our house was or how many of us my mother had to care for. I did not resent anything. I only knew that one day I would get out of there, move to the city, and do something big.

I look back on my memory of that village and my life there, and I wonder: given that kind of adversity and travail and hardship, how did I rise to where I am at today? What quality in my character causes me to rise above the hurdles life throws at me? How resolute is the human spirit! I marvel at the ability of people who grow up with such disadvantage to achieve outstanding things with their lives.

chapter thirteen

A History of the Man

"The best and most beautiful things in the world cannot be seen or even touched—they must be felt with the heart." —Helen Keller

I remember little about my childhood feelings and thoughts beyond playing on the shores of the Caribbean Sea, watching the waves, hearing the pleasant roar of the water, and enjoying the simple life in Anse La Raye, the little Saint Lucian village where I was born.

I grew up in a natural world, close to nature. Mine was a world without the trappings of technological wonders. As a boy, I had no access to TV, the Internet, phones, or motorized toys. My village's main road was a sandy pathway wide enough for two people to walk past each other.

There was not even running water. I remember clearly having to go down to the river to fetch buckets of water for our household to drink, cook with, bathe in, and wash the laundry. The river water was clean and pure back then. The river ran off the mountain and down to the sea. We lived close to the land. Trees were everywhere, streams flowed freely with fresh, clean water, and seafood and animals were easily available to fishers and hunters. We grew chicken and had our own egg-laying hens. It was an organic lifestyle. Everything was natural and easy to gather.

The poverty was visible only in the unpainted, neglected condition of the houses in the village, the lack of modern sanitation and utility services, and the worn-out clothes of the village people. There was no concept of paved roads or electricity or machines. We were people who lived simply off the land. Fruit was never bought. We could walk into our yard or down the laneway and pick mangoes, plums, coconut, banana, and countless other fruit right off the tree and eat it. Poverty for us did not mean starvation. The tropical land was blessed with natural food in abundance.

Ebb and Flow

I lived a simple life, an innocent life. As the eleventh of twelve children living with my parents, I can remember only that I would walk to school, come home, and do my homework and a few chores at home. Innocence pervaded my childhood. Even after my father died when I was fourteen, I accepted the ways of the world, unquestioning of fate.

My dad's death, however, shaped my worldview. I felt that I had to take on the burdens of the world. I have lived all my life with this sense of being responsible for everyone around me. I think I strive on this. When I was fourteen years old, my father died after a lengthy illness. He was bedridden for a few weeks before his death. He died with my mother and I and my eldest brother there with him in the room. The next day, my brother left us, not saying where he was going. Later, we found out that he had gone to England. I felt he had abandoned us. Although unable to articulate my feelings then, I suffered from a deep sense of abandonment and being left in the big world to fend for myself. But instead of facing that, I concentrated on my mother, on her sudden aloneness with no one there to support her with us, her twelve children. That is when I took on the responsibility for the family. I decided I would shoulder the burden.

All my life since then has been a taking on of burdens. The events of my life at fourteen years of age shaped my destiny in a profound way. Suddenly, at fourteen years of age I had to grow up and take the responsibility for the family.

My mother had also suddenly become the breadwinner in the family. My father used to be a farmer, and my mother was not about to go farming. She was a distinguished lady of French ancestry accustomed to the shelter of the home, away from the harshness of the hot sun. She was gifted as a housewife, mostly spending her days in the kitchen. She became a baker, making bread on brick stoves with old wood as fuel. After my father died, I took on the responsibility for the bakery operation. I would wake up at 4:00 a.m. with a smaller brother of mine and light up the stove and prepare it for my mother to start baking at 5:00 a.m.. By 6:00 a.m., enough bread was ready for my brother and I to go out in the village and sell, before time for school came at 8:30 a.m.. Our livelihood depended on how many pennies we made in the day from this fledgling bread business, which was more survival than business.

Now I sit in the management seat of my own business in Toronto, and that childhood has faded to the back of my mind, a distant memory. Yet the memory is filled with happy innocence, of the bright sun and the massive mountain and the wide-open sea and the roaring ways of nature. I lived close to the land,

A History of the Man

knowing the feel of sand and mud on the soles of my feet, feeling the wind caress my skin, loving the green trees swaying in the gentle Caribbean breeze.

Despite the size of my family, I hardly remember playing time with my siblings. Today, my family is all grown up, my youngest sister being fifty-five years old. Some have passed away. But I never experienced the closeness of family life. I was too busy taking on the burden of the family. Yet later in life I started wondering about my past, my ancestry. Who were my ancestors? Where did I come from?

My mother's name is Eudoxia. She got married at the tender age of seventeen. She was twenty years younger than my father, George, who died in his fifties and left the family of a dozen children and a poor woman to battle life. Today, I have two brothers alive and one sister, apart from myself. My family rode the waves of life facing great tragedies. But my family has also achieved astonishing accomplishments in Saint Lucia. We have become one of the new nation's enduring romantic stories, fighting through to break the barriers inherent in a young nation, to become one of the island's greatest families.

But the struggle has been tough. In 2003, a psychologically challenged man walked onto the farm of my eldest brother and murdered him. This mad man murdered my eldest brother on his estate. It was devastating to us. My brother had lived for many years in England before returning to Saint Lucia to settle down in his senior years, only to be murdered in a fit of madness. In fact, eight of my parents' children died before growing up. Only nine of us lived to adulthood.

My family probably descended from French plantation owners who came to the Caribbean during the colonial era. But I do not know any of my grandparents. I have no idea what my ancestry is, beyond my immediate family, my parents. When I was born on December 24, 1945, World War II was raging in Europe. But I grew up in the village in Saint Lucia called Anse La Raye in a big family, completely unaware of anything beyond the village. I had no idea of the war or of any life beyond Saint Lucia.

My mother ran a small shop on the muddy lane and a bakery, and my father was a farmer. From what I can remember, my early childhood was a nice life. There was less materialism. Life was simple, friendly and the village people were like one big extended family. Everyone lived like true neighbours. There was no crime or maliciousness that I can remember.

We swam in the Caribbean Sea as children. I grew up on the beach. I woke up in the morning, did a few chores like fetch water from the river for bathing,

Ebb and Flow

then went to school, came home and played in the sand on the shores of the sea. At night I did my homework by a small lamp fuelled with kerosene.

chapter fourteen

DISCIPLINE SHAPES CHARACTER

"Nearly all men can stand adversity, but if you want to test a man's character, give him power." —Abraham Lincoln

I remember my mother being a very strict disciplinarian. If anything defined my childhood, it was the disciplinary strictness of my mother, and the structured order of being an altar boy in the Catholic church.

The church building is the biggest structure in the village. It is now a massive stone artifice, grey and imposing against the backdrop of the village's rickety houses. My mother insisted that we as children be in church every Sunday. She made sure that we grew up following the Catholic creed.

I had to be on my best behaviour at all times. But this helped shaped my values and my work ethic. I know how to discipline myself to achieve a desired goal, because this was my life as a child. I had no choice but to live in this structured environment. It was carefree and open, but the social life that I had shaped me to develop a solid work ethic. The Catholic church was like that mountain in my mother's life—always there, strong and sturdy and steady—a permanent place of renewal and refreshing for life's harsh journey.

But the Caribbean is not about building something solid and sturdy. What dominates the landscape is not the mountain but rather the sea, with its shifting ebbs and flows, its constant movement. The Caribbean people have come to be defined by this innate desire to move on, to dance away the cares of building roots as a nation.

At an early age, I had to learn to deal with the migration issue. The Caribbean people came from a migrant culture. After Columbus discovered the islands in the fifteenth century, European agriculture lords shipped in African slaves, Indian indentured workers, Chinese labourers, and Portuguese workers to labour on the sugar, banana, and other agricultural plantations that made up the colonial economy.

Ebb and Flow

By the time political sovereignty came to the Caribbean from the 1960s through the 1980s, the Caribbean people had developed a sense of identity away from their ancestral origin. In fact, the Caribbean people had completely lost any sense of their ancestry. They had become a people literally with no history. And they made their own history over the centuries since their forced migration to the region. My family is a living example of this phenomenon. By the time my father died, I had three or four brothers who had migrated to England. I was at home with just two other siblings and my mom when he passed away. All the rest had created new lives for themselves, escaping from the cramped village as soon as they could.

So when my father died, as the eldest child still at home, I took on the role of family provider, a responsibility that I have adopted to this day. I love to feel that I am responsible for the world, starting with my immediate environment, but including the nation and the wider world. The ebb and flow of life has taught me to be responsible for others.

This rhythm of life—battling tragedy and migration while dreaming of escaping the little village life to the wide world beckoning beyond the horizon of the Caribbean Sea—has haunted me all my life. Finally, I myself migrated to Canada, taking my children and wife with me.

The tragedies of living in the Caribbean left me sore and beaten. A lot of my brothers and sisters had died. One brother died by drowning. My mother told me the story, because I was a baby when it happened. But my mother had to go through life facing all these things. She was a very strong person. And she taught us some solid life lessons. She taught us to respect other people, especially the elders. In fact, my mother was the main influence in my life. She was such a strict disciplinarian, but so was everybody around me. My teachers—the nuns—at the Catholic school whipped me so much that I really resented going to school. This environment of discipline really kept me along a straight and narrow path.

Even as I strived to conquer the forces that kept me from reaching my horizon, I knew that the social environment of my upbringing had given me the self-imposed boundaries that have kept me on the right path through my life. This environment of discipline included the priests at church, who would beat us if we talked during service.

Yet, I enjoyed my life in Anse La Raye as a boy. I still have friends from back there. My best friend today is from there. But he too has emigrated—to the British Virgin Islands.

chapter fifteen

THE SIMPLE RHYTHM OF LIFE

"The art of life is to know how to enjoy a little and to endure a lot."
—William Hazlitt

My family always had eyes turned towards the sea, longing for a life away from the little island. Beyond laid the realities of our dream, not there in the cramped village life of square box huts.

None of us even went to university. I left school at fourteen years of age. For one we were too poor, but also Saint Lucia back then was a very loving little country. People lived simply. My mom used to buy flour in white cotton bags to do her baking, and when the bags were empty, she would sew shirts for us out of the flour bag material. But I was so much happier then, so innocent.

My brother's wife still lives in the house where we grew up, in Anse La Raye.

Life has brought me through many trials and travails and triumphs since those innocent days. But today I manage the affairs of my hospitality business, and I have grown in wisdom and understanding, enough to realize that I cannot put value on my life based on my achievements. I look to go back to the simple way of living, to the innocence of not expecting much.

After leaving school at fourteen because my father had just died and I was responsible for the burdens of being provider to the family, I got a job at a sugar factory close to my village, distilling rum for $14 a fortnight. I missed my father. He was a nice man, very quiet. I spent a lot of time with him at the farm. And our family life at home was very good. My parents lived well with each other. And I always had a lot of friends. After school, we played outdoors till it was night, then we went in. I was really enjoying this innocence, and then it was shattered when my father died, though I still thought that this was just life and these things happen. Back then I did not question or challenge fate. I just took on the responsibilities of life.

Ebb and Flow

I had to go off to work at fifteen to help my mother after my father died. Since that first job, I have learned valuable life lessons, which I have determined to tell the world. My life story is a life lesson to anyone who strives to break out of their little village world to conquer the heady heights of business success on the world stage. I have done it. I know the road. And I want to share my wisdom and understanding with my children's generation.

To achieve success, you must have a determination and a willingness to achieve things. I strive to achieve success in life. And I got to the point where I could go back to that same poor little village, my Anse La Raye, and feed the poor people there. In fact, as a senator in the Saint Lucian senate, I dedicated all my salary to the village welfare. I put my salary in a special bank account for scholarships to the children of the village. I gave over twenty-five scholarships to children there for their secondary school education. I also supported the building of a community cultural centre in the village, and I renovated the Catholic church where I had served as an altar boy.

The road has not been easy. Escaping from the village took a lot of persevering. I joined the Royal Saint Lucia Police Force at the age of eighteen to escape from the little village life. I had failed the examinations a few times, but I kept at it, and eventually I passed and was accepted at the training school in Barbados. I finally was reaching for the horizon. After special training, I went back to serve the Saint Lucia nation as a policeman. I wanted to get out of the village. There was no future for me in the village or in the sugar factory distilling rum.

As early as eighteen years old, I had discovered the Caribbean curse: to strive for and reach the horizon of the Caribbean Dream, you have to migrate from where you are and reach beyond your community. This reality hit me as a teenager, and in my fifties I faced the same exact decision when I had to decide to leave Saint Lucia for a new life in Canada. The migration culture digs into the soul of the Caribbean Man, and he has to move on. And move on. And move on.

I worked as a policeman for three years, but constantly I was looking for bigger opportunities. That ambition that was born in my heart as I played on the edge of the Caribbean Sea, longing to know what lay beyond the distant horizon where the blue sky meets the blue sea, was never going to leave me. So, restless and pushing onward to bigger dreams, I quit the force when a businessman offered me a bigger salary and unlimited commission earning potential in an insurance company. I grabbed the opportunity with both hands, becoming an insurance salesman in the Saint Lucian capital, Castries.

The Simple Rhythm of Life

Meanwhile, I never left my faith world. My grounding in the Catholic church has seen me live a strong life of faith. My mother made sure I grew up in the church. And in my adult life, I faithfully attended mass every Sunday with my wife, Julia. Later, I repainted the church in my village and helped renovate it. I was a strong Catholic.

This life of discipline in my religion saw me channel the burning ambition in my heart to good use. I became one of Saint Lucia's pioneer developers, moving from a simple insurance salesman to owning the first life insurance company in the country. The Cadasse story is an amazing tale of triumph and overcoming.

chapter sixteen

THE VISION OF THE MAN

> *"Visual surprise is natural in the Caribbean; it comes with the landscape, and faced with its beauty, the sigh of history dissolves."*
> —Derek Walcott

Since I got married at the age of twenty-two, family life for myself has mostly been stable, peaceful, and enjoyable. Life throws up challenges wherever humans socialize, but despite the rough times, I have demonstrated a keen sense of family values. I got married at that young age to a lovely Saint Lucian lady named Julia. Over the years, we have raised five children—Ross, Kervin, Candace, Noel Jr., and Juli-Anne.

Ross works as an information technology recruiter, Kervin has a successful sales career, Candace works as an attorney, Noel Jr. is a Grammy-winning recording engineer, and Juli-Anne is a business analyst with a Fortune 500 company. We have done well by our children. We have seven grandchildren—Jada, Ross Jr., Anthony, Jonathan, Jedediah, Akeylah, and Amaya.

Considering what I have been through in my life in Saint Lucia, anyone else might have gone crazy or died. Instead, I am blessed. I feel so blessed and contented with life today. I am very contended and very happy, especially to have the family that I was blessed with.

Yet, I have worked hard for this contented happiness. Even when I joined the Royal Saint Lucia Police Force when I was eighteen years of age, it was not an easy road. My application to become a policeman was turned down several times, because I was too small in size. But I do not give up at all. Once I believe in a cause I pursue it. I pursued my dream of joining the force, and eventually I became the best drills officer at the training school in Barbados.

I attack the obstacles in life with fearless passion and self-confidence. I never have any fear in anything I do. I make decisions, and whatever the consequences,

Ebb and Flow

I am prepared to face them. In fact, if I lived my life over again, I would live the same way I did, except that I would really be more persistent to make sure I attended university. That's one thing I regret not being able to do.

However, I am a self-made man. I read widely, do a lot of self-study, participate in countless self-development seminars, have attended training programs at US universities sponsored by the Saint Lucian government, and listen to the wisdom and understanding of those who can teach me solid life lessons. I was not educated at university level because I had to quit school early, at fourteen. But I fear nothing, not even this lack of education in my life.

I still strived and reached for my dreams. I did not let anything hold me back. I rose to one of the highest political offices in Saint Lucia. I became a leader in my country. I can testify that if anyone takes his life seriously, no matter what negatives there may be, he or she can achieve outstanding success.

My most exciting moment was when I took my oath of office in parliament as a senator. I served as chairman of the Gaming Authority of Saint Lucia; I served as president of the Hotel and Tourism Association of Saint Lucia. Nothing is impossible to the one who believes he can accomplish his dreams. I am also honoured to be a life member of the Baron Institute and to have served as a Distinguished Lieutenant Governor of the Kiwanis Club International.

My approach to life allows me to accept things. I do not fight and stress. Even as a young boy, if I lost my marbles while playing with my friends, I did not cry or feel bad about it. I accept that life is the way it is, and we have to learn to get over stuff, move on, and make the most of our days.

One thing I could not accept, however, was how some people who I thought were my friends betrayed me after my political and business fallout. I really enjoyed politics. I remember standing in parliament and with great pomp and ceremony, slowly unbuttoning my jacket and squaring my shoulders, articulating every word slowly and deliberately. I would pontificate with pride to the parliament. That experience I enjoyed. Yet it developed in me pride and self-importance.

I am glad today that I am so humble. I remember a banker, Bob Dean, had advised me not to enter politics, because I am too soft, too nice a man, he said. As a politician, I opened my life to people. And people flocked around me, because they wanted to benefit from my position. I had always wanted to be in politics, and I used the position to help a lot of people and to live a very social life. I later regretted this tremendously. It was the cause of my downfall. I always reached out to people and tried to help too many. I reached out with a gener-

The Vision of the Man

ous heart to help others, and suffered for it. The Caribbean is prone to pettiness in politics. If too many people flock around a person, as they did to me because of my generous spirit, other political elites feel threatened.

But I know in my heart that I have a strong vision for Saint Lucia. I want to see every Saint Lucian enjoy a good lifestyle. I want to see my people have access to better health. Saint Lucia is too dependent on foreign handouts. I really do not think the country can be totally independent as a people. I do not see that happening in my lifetime.

I pushed for the government to allow local farmers preferential treatment to supply the hotels and tourism industry with local Saint Lucian produce. I was surprised how much opposition this idea received. However, in recent times there has been more cooperation between the tourism industry and the local agricultural sector. I am happy to see this.

My life has been a great success. And I want to see every Saint Lucian say that—that their life has been very successful. I have helped shape the lives of many people who crossed my path, especially when I was in business. I gave opportunities to many people in life—and I helped educate others, and push others into business.

I sponsored twenty-five scholarships for children in my home village of Anse La Raye, and throughout the country. I am ready to mentor a new generation of Caribbean leaders. I want to see people build solid relationships with each other and develop trust and love for each other. A friend is someone prepared to make sacrifices for you when called upon. This generation desperately needs this kind of relationship fostering.

I have known this kind of relationship with my wife. My happiest moment was the day I got married to Julia. We have been married for forty years, and she is such a tower of strength to me. I have had a great marriage. I have always believed that I have been blessed with my wife. She contributed enormously to my success. Today, young people are not preparing for long marriages. They do not know how to build lasting relationships. This is sad. The Caribbean suffers for it.

Young people today need to learn patience, tolerance, and the art of communication. This is very, very important. In my generation, although I grew up poor and so innocent, I was able to achieve great success. I had a very fortunate life. I was making money and contributing to the development of my country. Then, alas, I went into politics. That really opened my eyes to the reason why the Caribbean is still a place where its people suffer and want to emigrate.

chapter seventeen

THE POLITICAL EXPERIENCE

"Every man I met is my superior in some way. In that, I learn of him."
—Ralph Waldo Emerson

As vice president of the St. Lucia Labour Party and then acting chairman, appointed in 1995, I enjoyed political life. I enjoyed chairing party meetings, and when I saw the passion in those meetings, I learned the inside working of politics and understood the machinations that go on in politics.

I learned about the underhanded lobbying of people trying to attract the attention of would-be parliamentarians. It gave me a sound understanding of party politics, how people attached some sort of meaning to everything spoken from the lips of a politician. I felt that I had no real freedom of speech to really authentically express myself. Whatever I said was taken in the wrong context. It was a game. But it never bothered me then. I was living to satisfy a public image. It was not difficult for me to fit into the political spectrum. It was very, very easy to be in the political limelight. I enjoyed it too.

I recall a situation when the prime minister wanted the senate to ratify a bill that had passed through parliament involving a substantial amount of money loaned by government to a failing private airline to keep it afloat. Several senators refused to support the bill. Three of those senators were fired. I felt these senators were justified in voting against the bill. In my loyalty to the government, to the country, and to the cause, I voted for the bill, which was passed in the senate. This went against my conscience. The airline failed anyway. The basis for the three senators voting against the bill was justified. I regret that I did not follow those senators and vote with my conscience.

The government asked me to become chairman of the gaming commission. This was a potentially powerful post, and so to take it up, I had to resign as senator. I was the first chairman of the Saint Lucia Gaming Authority. In this position,

Ebb and Flow

I set up the institutional infrastructure for the administration and management of that area of the tourism sector. I was asked to give up my parliamentary position to become the commissioner, but it turned out to be a way for the government to get rid of me. It was the start of my decline and fall.

When politicians are seeking power, they try to please everyone, even those who are wrong, by justifying the wrong, making it look right to garner support and loyalty. We start with good intentions. Most politicians come in with good intentions, but the system corrupts them very quickly. The only way to change the system is by having the economic power to effect change. Most politicians, especially in the Caribbean, are poorer than a lot of the people they serve when in power. So they subject themselves to those who have more economic power, and that is what has held back the progress of the smaller islands.

At the end of the day, economic power is more valuable than political power. I learned this being in politics. Politics is not for me. I did not find honesty in the politicians that I served with. The sincerity of purpose that politicians claim they stand for was absent. In fact, there was a minister of tourism who asked me to suggest to him a board of directors, since he was nominating me to be the chairman of the Saint Lucia Tourist Board. Within twenty-four hours, I was flabbergasted to hear on national radio that he had appointed a new chairman and had already selected a board. I found that dishonest and highly unethical.

When you are successful, you inevitably step on people's toes and hurt them, many times without realizing it. You are not at all aware you are hurting people. And when you are down, these people come like sharks to attack you in your weakest moment. Even my best friend at the time—a man I had trained and helped develop and given a big job with my company, a man I liked a lot—turned against me. In public life, your persona becomes public domain. The newspapers discover your name and your success. And there suddenly appear people who want to tear you down, for no reason other than petty jealousy or sly envy. The main cause of my fall was because of getting into public life.

I lived a vision for Saint Lucia. I had a deep commitment to tourism. I wanted to make a difference politically through bringing the tourism and agriculture state ministries together. But I could not achieve this vision, which would have helped families all over the land. I could not achieve it, because I feel that my political position was merely in title and name, not in substance. Tourism now is the leading economic sector that drives the GDP.

The perennial story of the Caribbean was playing itself out, and the dream of being free from the colonial masters was turning into a bitter nightmare for

The Political Experience

me, a dedicated son of the Caribbean—a man who had dreamed as a boy on the shores of the Caribbean Sea in the little village of Anse La Raye, that one day I would help eradicate the poverty of Saint Lucia that had robbed me of a proper childhood and left my parents facing one tragedy after another.

Today, I manage the affairs of my new business with efficiency and love. But my mind constantly focuses on Saint Lucia, thinking about the fifty-eight years that I invested in my homeland, only to see it all vanish before I could grow old and enjoy the fruits of my labour.

A nation of people cannot develop unless it takes care of its own. And I had learned that when you are down and out in the Caribbean, no one binds your wounds and nurtures your sores. So with a bleeding heart, I emigrated to a place where I can live the rest of my days in quiet enjoyment of my own inner contentment and peace, cradled in the arms of my family and my God.

chapter eighteen

THE AFFLICTIONS OF THE MAN

"Making your mark on the world is hard. If it were easy, everybody would do it. But it's not. It takes patience. It takes commitment, and it comes with plenty of failure along the way. The real test is not whether you avoid this failure, because you won't. It's whether you let it harden or shame you into inaction, or whether you learn from it: whether you choose to persevere." —Barack Obama

I know the travails that haunt life on this earth.

On May 31, 2008, I came to work at my office at the business place, the La Villa Banquet and Convention Centre in Toronto, Canada. I got up as usual and made my way around the main hall, walking, feeling fine. However, on my way back to the office, in a split second I blacked out and fell limp to the floor.

My fall caused me to hit my head on the marble floor, and I suffered a gashing wound. I don't know what happened. I was out. I learned later that a staff member called emergency and an ambulance came and took me to hospital. I received twenty-four stitches on my head. The scar is there on my scalp. I spent four days in the hospital. But I came out and resumed my work, not having any idea that this would keep reoccurring. The falls kept happening. I would be walking, feeling okay, and suddenly I would just crumble and collapse on the floor.

This time of adversity and such health challenges created in me the desire to fight on, to win. I still have so much to do. I want to make this business the resounding success I have envisioned for it. For I am a man who never gives up, despite the gravest of adversity that comes my way.

I have proven to myself that I have the ability to scale any height to overcome any obstacle. I was only a child when my father died in Anse-La-Raye, the tiny, poverty-stricken village in Saint Lucia.

Ebb and Flow

Yet I grew up to become chairman of the governing political party before I was fifty years old. In fact, I became chairman of local government for the community where I grew up at the tender age of twenty-two years. As head of the village, my role was akin to that of mayor of a municipality.

Now in my sixties, I was starting a new multi-million dollar business, and my physical health was giving up on me. The first time I fell, we had 600 people at a Pentecostal church revival service at the banquet hall. The church had booked their event for that evening, and I was overseeing the event. I had to be rushed to the hospital in the middle of it. I felt helpless.

With my business partner, Cory Mills, I had bought the La Villa Banquet and Convention Centre after my business partnership with another businessman at another banquet hall had gone sour. There was a huge breakdown in that partnership, and I was just getting back on my feet with this new venture when my physical health got worse and worse.

I took over the management and ownership of La Villa on December 7, 2007, thus enlarging my responsibility. Before, at the last business, I was managing a 700-seat capacity business. Now I had a 1,000-seat capacity hospitality business to manage. I moved from a small plaza locale to a 40,000-square-foot building on a two-and-a-half acre property. In the six months between the two ventures, I went from being devastated that I had lost to being elated that I could create this breakthrough that was so much bigger than my last. I was amazed at how gracious the Lord is to me, to grant me this opportunity to do something bigger.

The day that I got the keys to the business in my hands, I thanked the Lord because I realized how much He was blessing me. I am convinced beyond any doubt that it was divine intervention. But I had learned that life is not a smooth road. And the lessons I had learned along the way prepared me for the adversity that was starting to afflict my physical health.

The collapse of the business partnership would have left a less courageous man beaten and broken. But God's grace was with me. Despite facing such challenges as having to close the mortgage to acquire my new residence at the same time my business partnership was turning negative, I persevered, never thinking to give up, that life for me was over. I always live knowing that God closes doors and He opens doors. My faith has carried me through life.

I have faced unbelievable misfortunes, setbacks, and extremely challenging obstacles. But as one door would shut, leaving me standing outside in trauma, another door would open with greater opportunity. Instead of me

The Afflictions of the Man

growing bitter and wallowing in self-pity, I am actually becoming more and more confident and positive. It is quite an amazing journey.

Although I have come to learn that there is a new, exciting chapter ahead and that the old gives way to new things, I have had to battle many demons: I have contemplated suicide; I have had days when all the negative stuff that happened to me from my childhood to my senior years has played over and over in my mind; I have felt like I was losing the will to continue in the battle of life.

But one of the winning formulas for me has been my support structure. I have built up a system in my life that allows me to come out a winner, always. My wife, Julia, and my daughter, Juli-Anne, have totally and unequivocally supported me, without reservation and without conditions, throughout my trials, talking to me, caring for me.

One day my wife told me about the Biblical story of Job, and that encouraged my heart. Job had faced such adverse circumstances and trials, yet he overcame and became successful again. The story of Job, reiterated to me over and over by my wife and daughter, encouraged me and pushed me to search for new opportunities.

Out of this search for new opportunities, I found the La Villa Banquet and Convention Centre, and I was able to negotiate with a business bank and the vendor to work out a favourable and workable deal to purchase the business.

I remember how the opportunity was secured. I went to my lawyer to draft my last will and testament, and in the process of doing that I shared with him my desire to own the banquet hall. Right then and there he offered to partner with me. It was the start of a new beginning. Just like so many times before, God had granted me His grace to once again rise to the challenge, to produce amazing results.

I borrowed money from friends, worked tirelessly to enrol the bank into the project, and persuaded the vendor to accept my proposal for purchasing the business, including the property. With my family fully on board supporting and strengthening me; with financing in place and a business partner willing to step in and play a dynamic role in the venture; with the exciting new future wide open in front of me, I walked into the new office, sat down at the desk, and picked up the phone: I was on the way to creating an even bigger success story than I had thought possible even three months before.

My family has always reminded me of my capacity to come back, to get back up when I fall. You should never stop living—you must continue to serve in whatever capacity you find inspiring, until your last breath. I believe I can serve society in the hospitality business. I am committed to this life of service in this industry. And I have learned that you just do not ever give up. In this business I am making a fantastic contribution to the community. Through my entrepreneurship, I create jobs, help charities, and provide a satisfying experience for social and family events. This gives me great satisfaction.

I have lived my life as a provider, taking on the burden of building businesses to employ people and provide a safe network of economic activity. I live my life to make money, to take control of my destiny, and I direct my energies to providing economic stimulus that creates a sound living standard for people in my community. I am committed to economic well-being.

I have faced feelings of hurt, betrayal, and failure—frequently blaming myself for things not going well. I tend to take personal responsibility when things do not go well, for whatever happens.

Then my health started failing me. There I was, in a hospital bed. And all I could think of was the business. I received the twenty-four stitches to my head, got discharged from the hospital, and went right back to the office to run the business. In the next three months I would fall six more times, the last of which resulted in me being rushed by ambulance back to the emergency room. That last fall occurred in August 2008.

Immediately, I was put into an operating room for heart tests. The results were shocking: I was having heart stoppages—my heart would literally stop beating for eight seconds, causing me to black out. I endured all sorts of testing, including carrying a medical heart monitoring device on my chest for two days.

The news was not good. The test results saw me immediately admitted to hospital for specialist heart treatment. The intention was to implant a pacemaker to aid my heart. The pacemaker did not help. Six weeks after the pacemaker was installed inside my chest, I suffered a major heart attack in my bed, while I slept. Julia, my wife, and Juli-Anne, who live with me at our comfortable Mississauga home in Ontario, Canada, immediately took me to the hospital. Within hours I was identified as a major heart risk and earmarked for a quadruple bypass heart surgery.

Adversity, falling on hard times, is not something new to me. In my political and business ventures in Saint Lucia, I believe there was a conspiracy to undermine me—both from my political colleagues and some business competitors, whom I once thought were my friends.

I believe that the prime minister I had the honour to serve with tacitly endorsed my demise by his actions. I was the sacrificial lamb on the altar of

The Afflictions of the Man

transparency. The government was preaching something they never practiced—accountability. I felt that the prime minister never kept to his word, in my opinion making promises he never kept. I felt that he operated with clandestine unscrupulousness. They used me. They still owe my business a substantial amount of money. I regret my decision to get involved in active politics.

When I served as president of the Hotel and Tourism Association and a director of the Saint Lucia Tourist Board, then-prime minister Vaughn Lewis in 1996 accused me of making uncomplimentary statements about him and demanded I make a public apology.

I had asked the prime minister if he would give the main address at the annual general meeting luncheon of the Tourism Association. But instead, he demanded a public apology from me, to be made on national television, before he would accept the speaking engagement. Against this background I felt humiliated. I felt he had robbed me of my freedom of expression, that he had used the big stick of his office.

While I concurred and apologized to the prime minister on national TV, it has up to this day left me sad and bitter. For I knew I had said nothing derogatory or uncomplimentary of the prime minster. I apologized on national TV in the interest of my association, and he then decided to address the association luncheon, an address which I considered to be pathetic because there was no substance in his address on the policy and direction of his government towards tourism.

After the Vaughn Lewis incident where I was virtually forced to apologize to the prime minister on public television, I got disappointed. Even as he was speaking to me behind the scenes to be a candidate for his party, he treated me like that. At that time I held him in high esteem, because he was the director general of the Organization of Eastern Caribbean States. We got on well. On several occasions he was guest speaker for the hotel association. So it was a usual protocol to invite him to give the feature address. Therefore, I considered his behaviour petty, and it was not fitting for me to serve under his leadership. So I decided instead to join the opposition Saint Lucia Labour Party.

I decided I wanted to make a contribution to the nation, and so I took action and got into politics. From the time I was in my early thirties I had political ambitions. I had first approached former leader of the Saint Lucia Labour Party, Dr. Julian Hunte, to run for the Labour Party. But he had chosen another man, a teacher from my district. For the record, Julian Hunte never became prime minister.

Ebb and Flow

I feel that former prime minister Vaughn Lewis, as a result of the petty behaviour demonstrated towards me, does not have the leadership qualities to be considered a great Caribbean leader, or even an iconic Saint Lucian leader. He cannot find a political place in a country that he claimed to have loved. A man who was that vindictive to me in high office can never be great in that office. No leader in the Caribbean ought to have behaved that way. It was small minded and petty—and that is what the Caribbean seems to be today. Saint Lucia is a microcosm of the political state of the entire Caribbean.

This is what is holding us back as a people. We have good people of talent, knowledge, and intelligence right around the Caribbean and some of the best brains that are serving the world. These brains could come back and serve the region.

The leadership of the Caribbean needs to recognize the role that indigenous expatriates can play in the region's development and implement policies to attract and encourage these sons and daughters of the soil to return home and contribute to the social and economic development of the people.

But these are adversities that I had to face. And so for me to face the health problems today, I draw a lot of strength from what I have already gone through in life. Most of all, I draw strength from my unshaken faith in the Lord Jesus Christ.

Today, I have undergone a quadruple bypass surgery; I receive daily medication for diabetes; I have to visit the dialysis centre three times a week for treatment; I am on a waiting list for a new kidney. Yet I operate the business on a full-time basis, ably supported by my wife.

I continue to deal with the ebbs and flows of this life, determined not to be beaten, but to come out victorious and triumphant. I live a thankful and grateful life, facing every obstacle with the strength of resolve that comes from a life striving to overcome all odds and every obstacle.

chapter nineteen

HOW THE TROUBLES BEGAN

"I don't believe in failure. It's not failure if you enjoyed the process."
—Oprah Winfrey

In 1997, when the Saint Lucia Labour Party won the election that launched it into political power, I was at the top of my game. I was appointed to the senate, I owned several businesses, I lived in my dream home and I was enjoying all of the accoutrements that came with living life in the political limelight. All of this was to be short-lived and I would soon find this out in the most traumatic and humiliating way.

My service to the Saint Lucia Labour Party had come at the expense of my businesses. The time I devoted to travel and handle the affairs of the party meant time away from my usual hands on involvement with the daily operations of the businesses that I had worked hard all my life to establish. I was intelligent enough to recognize this fact, but I was making a conscious and calculated risk assuming that the benefits would outweigh any potential temporary losses. After all, where there is politics, there are promises and promises were made to me.

The repercussions of all the neglect of my business became apparent in 2001. The hotel business began declining first, and became a heavy financial burden on the insurance business, which owned it. I approached the Prime Minister with a plan to separate the two businesses from each other, but I needed the support and backing of the National Bank which held the mortgage in order to be able to do so. He promised to discuss the matter with the bank but to my knowledge he never did.

The bank eventually seized the hotel and they did so in an epic and unprecedented way. Although neither I nor my son who served as general manager at the time had police records, the Special Services Unit (SSU)—an arm of the police force which deals with hard criminals—was sent to escort us off the property.

This moment was terribly traumatizing and humiliating for me. I felt that my world had collapsed. I said nothing and quietly walked out. By the time I drove the few minutes to get to my home at Rodney Bay, the story of my sudden and unexpected misfortune was all over the national news. When I got home, my family had already heard what happened.

I felt alone in the world, with no one to turn to. I was in shock. It took a few days for the events to settle in and for me to wrap my mind around this reality.

As a result of the loss of the hotel, I was eventually forced to sell the insurance company to Guyana and Trinidad Mutual Life Assurance Company. This was another great loss but not the last that I would experience.

My 3 million dollar home went into receivership next. From an early age, as soon as I got married at age twenty-two, I started to save to build this home. I changed homes three or four times before I was able to make it a reality. It was a 7,000 square foot palatial residence situated in the most elite part of the country—the Rodney Bay area. I had built it from the ground up with blood, sweat and tears. This is the house where I hosted all of the friends, many of whom turned out to be enemies in the end. I had lived there for sixteen years with my family when we lost it.

Incidentally, the financial institution that seized my home was a company that I worked with for nineteen years. I had fallen out with the general manager because I had to write him a letter, reprimanding him for his conduct in fraternizing intimately with many of the staff members in the Saint Lucia branch office for which I had responsibility as the branch manager. The board fired me as a result. At the time that I was fired, I had just won a company competition where I was awarded a trophy and a $7,000 bonus, so I knew that I was not being terminated for professional inability, but because of the letter that I had written about my staff, which was likely perceived as insubordination.

I had served the government faithfully, I never had a problem either with the party or the government, but my business suffered. My integrity and character were never in question. But I left my business to other people to run while I was gallivanting all around the world on behalf of the party. This inevitably led to the demise of my business empire. And when I turned to the party and the government for assistance, all I got was a cold shoulder, eventually being left out in the cold to deal with things myself. I felt abandoned.

How the Troubles Began

Now that I had lost everything and these business associates had disappointed me I was looking for a job to sustain myself and my family. I remember that I was negotiating for employment with several companies and, while offering me great opportunities for to work with them after I had closed down my business, they were actually making me a fool, having no intention of employing me or offering me any opportunity. Rather discourteously and unceremoniously, they treated me with gross disrespect.

The general manager of a company took me to lunch and offered me to be his executive sales director. Then another company owner offered me a consultancy job to develop and train people to set up a new insurance company for him. He was attempting to open his own motor insurance company. I did the institutional requirement. All he had to do was get the license. He instead gave the job to someone who had been my former employee in my own business.

Then there was another company, whose owner wanted me to be the executive director for his group of companies. On the day I was supposed to start the job he ordered me to take a van and go around the country and the hotels and sell spices and milk products.

It was another attempt to humiliate me given the fact that I had just lost my business as the CEO and had also fallen out of grace with the government and Prime Minister Kenny Anthony, who had unceremoniously terminated my appointment as the Chairman of the Gaming Authority.

My entire investment into the socio-economic development of my homeland, Saint Lucia, ended in this bitterness because of my involvement in politics and the unfulfilled promises of those who I had helped to gain political power in the interest of the progress of the nation. I knew that I had to leave the country. Thankfully and I believe by divine providence, I had a place to go.

In 1981, my family was young and my children were growing, but Saint Lucia was in turmoil. There was looting and political fear in Saint Lucia due to a political riot over a power struggle. The whole city was devastated. Any sane thinking man then wanted just to leave the country. The then Prime Minister Allan Louisy had ousted the late Sir John Compton and the country descended into chaos.

At that time I had an opportunity to apply for Canadian citizenship and so I went to Edmonton, Alberta with my family to do so. I eventually received my citizenship in 1987 and was able to secure landed immigrant status for my entire family. We became dual citizens. Canada became a refuge for me and my family in the wake of my demise.

Ebb and Flow

On May 11 2003 I woke up on a sunny day that I will never forget. Julia and I woke up early in the morning and had breakfast, picked up our bags, went to the airport by taxi and headed for Canada leaving all our belongings behind in our home at Rodney Bay. Since then we have never been back to Saint Lucia. I was fifty-eight years old when I left Saint Lucia permanently for Canada. Though I knew it was necessary, there was a serious conflict, a serious dichotomy, in my spirit when I left. Still, I have no regrets about what happened to me. I look back now with thankfulness at all that happened. While it was bitter at the time, today I hold no grudges against anyone. I was a political figure. It was not personal. I have come to understand that it comes with the territory.

With the experience I have today I would not advise any of my family to go into politics. But if I had to re-live my life I would do what I did, both for the party and the country that I love so dearly.

My family is prominent and well-known in Saint Lucia. My whole family has been well-respected and supported the community in business and charity. My brother owns one of the leading bakeries in Castries. I was the baker of the family, which I did after my father died, with another brother. We turned that experience into a family business.

This book spans fifty years of one man's life, looking at the world from my experiences. I want to leave a legacy of service, kindness and be known as a person who has had a big heart. I think right now I have that legacy. I have accomplished a lot of my dreams. All that is left is to serve the Lord. God has spared me. There are many people all over the world. Some people are dying. People are out there without arms, legs, or eyes. I am totally contented and happy. For the Lord has been good to me. I know the Lord has blessed me. I thank Him every day.

chapter twenty

Concluding Thoughts

"Only a life lived for others is a life worthwhile." —Albert Einstein

Saint Lucia found itself in the latter half of 2007 in the grip of a deep political crisis. The political father of the nation—Sir John Compton, who had led us to political independence from the British Empire in 1979—passed away while he was serving as prime minister.

That event plunged the nation into a leadership crisis that I had warned about since the early 1990s. My own political demise, which claimed my business ventures and my family life, causing me to have to emigrate to Canada, stemmed from the national characteristic of the leaders of this small Caribbean island state. The leaders seem too interested in power grabs for themselves. There is a lack of teamwork ability and no interest in putting the nation above personal gains. We as a nation must mature beyond this.

Some things in life you just cannot understand. But you just go along and accept life and just live. Human beings are always, I believe, under the divine hand of Providence. So we just have to live by faith. Yet we have control of our own destiny. We can, and must, strive to improve our society. We have the responsibility to rise up and lead the next generation into a better future, a more secured community, where they can achieve their dreams.

But like a child growing up in the country and moving suddenly to a big city, exposed to seeing the bright lights of glamour, we become overwhelmed—we keep playing with the switch, not realizing how dangerous it can be. That's how life is for most of us. Sometimes we even damage the switch because we do not know better. We want only to experience the highs of adventure, with little regard for future consequences.

When you have gone through a situation, it is only then that understanding comes. Understanding comes from experiencing life. Experience is indeed the greatest teacher in life. And Saint Lucia is yet a young nation. It is still going through the experience of growing up as a nation.

But individually, you must understand that whatever happens to you in life, you must train yourself not to be bitter about your circumstances. It could consume you and it can rob you of the joy of life.

I have had to let go and forgive everyone who contributed to my demise. The key is to never let circumstances consume you and lead to bitterness within. People have a tendency to become vindictive. But it is your ability to rise above self-absorption and to see life in its true form, where there is a greater joy in life than holding on to pain inflicted by others.

The essence of living life is to do the best that you can and live at peace with all men. You have to strive for this. Live righteously. It comes from your conscience, knowing that you are not hurting anyone at all. It took me many years and lots of sleepless nights to find this out.

Many times I thought of committing suicide. I thought I was a failure. But when I found the Lord Jesus Christ as Saviour and Lord, I realized that we own nothing in this world. We are just the custodians of the world's wealth for a time. Before that realization, I had thought my whole purpose was to acquire wealth.

Today my paradigm has shifted. I want to help people more, to reach out to others and help them live better lives and find joy in their daily living. Before, I had a lot of issues. Now I have no issues at all. Transformation takes place in your life when you go through loss. You are no longer a slave to material stuff. You must know how to resign everything to His hands—then you acquire that state of mind that is so important to living successfully and to help build a good society.

It's an inner peace and joy that you achieve, which is unexplainable. I achieved this only after I lost everything in Saint Lucia. I would like to admit that. Success makes you arrogant and prideful, because people around you make you feel like a god handing out goodies. But when the challenges come, you have to realize that you are human and you do not really have any power. In politics, in the moment of a vote, you can become nothing.

So my goal now is to enjoy the evening of my years and to teach as many young people as I can about life. I have learned a lot through the years. My experiences have taught me tremendous wisdom and understanding. I want to share this with the world. I want to make a positive and good impact on my fellow humans. If I can help one person enjoy life, I will be happy.

Concluding Thoughts

I remember the encouragement I got back in Saint Lucia from Pastor McLaurens. He came to Toronto for a visit recently and spent a week with me. He was there for me when I had need for someone to talk to me, to pray with me, to encourage me. He was not there because of who I was or my circumstances, but because he lives to help other people enjoy their life. That's how I strive to live my life today—to be there as an encourager and comfort to all those who need a shoulder to lean on or words of comfort and care.

I remember people like Michael White, who helped me and mentored me through my crisis. The Lord sent these people to me in my hour of need. I am now available for the Lord to send me to others who need such people in their lives. White counselled me and prayed with me every day. I have learned the value of what that means.

In the Caribbean, superstition is rife, and the pastor had to help me fight off evil. People were actually plotting witchcraft against my family and I. I found blood sacrifices on the floor of my bakeries several times when I turned up in the mornings to open the place for business. We just used to wash it off, not realizing what was going on. I had enemies and I did not even know. I did not know why I had these enemies, but I was not scared or concerned. I just carried on. I took it very lightly. But I can look back now and realize that God was protecting me from these enemies, who would go to any means to destroy someone they envy.

Think of it, I could have become worse for those demonic attacks. They were evil. But now I know, with thanksgiving in my heart, that God was there protecting me. He is here now. My life is in His hands. Even family had turned against me back then. I felt there was a conspiracy against me, bent on bringing me down.

But my wife, Julia, was always there for me. She is such a strong woman of faith. People were even advising her to leave me, but she never did. She stuck with me through all my failures and faults. She watched her entire lifestyle collapse. It was very hard for her. All our children worked in the businesses that I owned.

The day the police showed up at our hotel and escorted my son and myself out of our own business place was the most devastating for myself and my family, especially Julia. But she persevered and supported me all the way to where we are today. These were the most elite police in the country, and they were armed to the hilt. The financial institution had moved against us, and our beloved Caribbees Hotel had gone into receivership.

Ebb and Flow

The team that took over the management and who were in charge of turning the hotel around appointed someone who was my business associate and my best friend. She was so close to me that I counted her as my best friend. Even the night before, she and I socialized and she never told me that they were going to move against me the next day, although she knew. That experience knocked my confidence in people. It left me bitter and cold. How can you trust people, and then they turn so drastically against you?

Soon after, this person became a dismal failure in the hotel business, and our hotel was sold off to a foreign company. Saint Lucia had again lost a piece of its soul to petty envy and jealousy. The nation had again become victim of deceit and insincerity. This is the story of the small states of the Caribbean. People aspire to leadership not because they have a genuine desire to help the nation rise to its glory, but to grab whatever they can, from whomever they can.

Imagine. A good friend of mine, whom I trusted and wined and dined, who had enjoyed the fine hospitality of my home as a trusted friend and colleague, had now conspired against me. I was bitter and hurt. It took me years, but I have learned to forgive this person. But definitely that was the end of our friendship.

Yet I have grown to realize that I am not being run by man, by the forces of circumstances in this world. My life is in the hands of Almighty God. I function purely by the wisdom and blessing of the Lord.

It is very, very painful to lose everything in life—the material stuff—but also to lose everyone, my family and friends who were closest to me. This was painful. You trust people. And when they turn against you, all of life turns upside down. But I know my conscience is clear, because I was not guilty in disturbing any strained relationship. These were people I had trained and helped give a career to in my businesses. Even my brother, who was a transportation conductor in London, England, when I brought him home to Saint Lucia and built a successful bakery for him, I gave it all to him.

I know that I did nothing wrong to people. I have tried my best to improve the lives of those around me. I did good for people, and a lot of them turned against me. People could be very ungrateful, and they have short memories.

I once helped the prime minister, Dr. Kenny Anthony, who once told me he could not pay his rent. This was before he got into political office. I gave him money—helped him financially. In fact, to help the Saint Lucia Labour Party get into power—and Dr. Anthony to become prime minister—I spent over $75,000 US of my own money.

Concluding Thoughts

These things do not bother me now. I have faith in God that I will be exonerated fully. I have seen the work of the Lord.

I have come to recognize that the higher up the ladder of success you climb, the heavier you fall. And there are people waiting at the bottom to see you stumble, so they can hasten your fall. It is the nature of this sinful world that we live in.

But God knows us. And He protects us and provides for us. For example, I had no idea that my life in Saint Lucia would collapse so spectacularly. Yet way back in 1981, I applied for Canadian citizenship. I had no reason to do that then. But God knew that twenty years later I would need that blessing to overcome the petty climate prevailing in Saint Lucia.

Today, I see the Almighty's hand in guiding me way back then, when I did not know why, to do this. I just woke up one morning and went to the Canadian Embassy and applied and got citizenship. Back then I had no idea that I was actually investing in my future. This is the result of a life lived for the Lord, with your heart pure before Him. God knew that twenty-five years later, in the future, I would need this move to Canada. Just trust God with your life.

When my business collapsed and I was kicked out of the political process in Saint Lucia, my children felt the loss. They were saddened, but they have so much confidence in me, their father. They fully supported me. And today I have so much to be thankful for. The history has been written. History is history. I cannot cry over spilled milk. We are called to get up and move on, live on, seize the new day, and make the most of it. Yesterday is gone. Leave it alone and look to the future and strive for what you know you can achieve.

chapter twenty-one

CONCLUDING ADVICE

"We must not allow ourselves to become like the system we oppose."
—Bishop Desmond Tutu

When I lost so much in such a short time in Saint Lucia, my doctor advised me that I should leave the country and recuperate elsewhere. I was so shattered and broken. I discussed the situation with the doctor, and he told me to get out as soon as possible and relocate. It was humanly impossible for any man to survive under that enormous amount of stress.

I never had that kind of stress in my life before. It was the worse couple years in my whole life. For the first time in my life, I felt what it was to be at the bottom of society's ladder. I felt so alone. There was no friend, no family apart from my wife and children who stood by me.

In fact, migrating from the Caribbean to North America was the last thing on my mind. But my family supported the decision to move. I had a lot of mixed feelings when I left. It was May 11, 2003. I turned my back and left. I have never been back. All I took was my overnight bag. I was fifty-five years old. I left my homeland. And in Canada, I felt like I was being tortured.

For the first year, it was really hard being away from what I had known all my life as home. I never wanted to leave. But by 2002, I realized that there was nothing there for me. I had to leave. That is where the Caribbean stands today. Its people have to leave. They find it too difficult to achieve their dreams in their own homeland, so they seek greener pastures in North America.

But my nation has always been a migrant people. I do not know my grandparents. We were a people without roots. I had tried to build roots, to develop over the years a business culture in Saint Lucia. But the system uprooted me and left me bare and exposed to the harsh reality of a people who do not know how to build their own history in their own land.

Ebb and Flow

So I came from this place of no roots, no ancestry. My parents were all immigrants from Africa and Europe. I was the second generation in my family to occupy this island state that used to be home to British plantation slaves. And I could not build roots there. I had to leave, move on, and continue the tradition of migration.

I came to Canada, and I could not even get a job. I had no Canadian experience, they said. I started selling water coolers house to house. I felt so much humiliation. To fall from being a senator in a powerful government to become a door-to-door salesman in Toronto was very humbling for me. And I sold just one policy. After that, I tried selling other products door to door: again, humiliation. I tried network marketing in the health industry, and that fell through. Then, in 2005, two years after I arrived, I finally got a job at a banquet hall in the hospitality industry, for which I have so much experience and knowledge.

That job was the turning point of my life. I made a proposal to a businessman to take his health product and network marketing strategy to the Caribbean. I worked on that for a while, but I moved on to bigger things when I was able to acquire a banquet hall.

Today, I am a happy and contented man. In this world, it is not the hard times that can knock you down but the way you handle circumstances. It is not the amount of falls you take. Rather, it is your ability to get up again and battle on, believing that you are destined to live a life of worth, purpose, and substance.

I am myself amazed that God has given me the opportunity to rise again like this. But we all have the opportunity to never give up—to believe and trust Him and strive constantly to achieve our dreams. I genuinely resigned myself to God's destiny for me. I gave up fighting and left things to His divine will. And today I am happier for that decision. My wife and I pray together, and we have surrendered to the Lord. I should state here emphatically that my spirituality has been completely resuscitated.

I used to depend on my daughter's wage to survive. My children and I have a strong bond. Now they see that their father is doing well in life again, and they rejoice for me. They have seen me fall and rise again. It is a good life lesson for them. They have now all accepted Jesus Christ as Lord and Saviour.

Life is about perseverance, never giving up—about totally believing that you can do big things with your days on this earth.

We who are born in the Caribbean have to deal with the institutionalized culture that fosters complacency. Though the region has advanced a lot in the past twenty years, the mentality of the leadership class still strives on power

Concluding Advice

grabs. What happened to me was that I made very poor judgments, and the region does not allow for human failures. A failure in the Caribbean is devastating. There is no second chance. It's like the sharks are waiting to eat you up when you bleed. We need to develop to a point where we have a system of support for those who dare to build the society into something more.

My fall did not happen overnight. Over a twenty-five-year period, my poor judgments added up, culminating in my final demise. The road was long and hard for me to grow and build a business and to try to impact the society through politics. I want to see these small countries have better support systems to help those who are visionary to achieve their plans and purposes.

I was a guy who wanted to please everyone and be nice to everybody. But it is better to be genuine and honest with people, and face their displeasure, than to try to be a "good guy" to everyone and end up with everyone stabbing you in the back.

I took a lot of chances, delved into several businesses, trusting partnerships that never worked. But today I am much more matured. I am not at all materialistic. My quality of life today is driven by family values. What defines me today is different. Today I am a man who has done it all and I am seeking the Lord and loving people and doing things that are more meaningful for the people around me than before. Before, I expected returns from what I did for others. Today I do things purely from the joy of sharing.

As a young person you are trained and shaped by your environmental influences such as family, friends, media, social situations, etc. You react to what is going on around you. You want to be like the world. This breeds an environment that fosters envy and jealousy. Deep within us we are conditioned to be envious and jealous for what others have that we do not. We push ourselves for what our neighbours have, but we find that the striving for material gain just because "they" have it to be too much, because that is not what we need. We just want to have things for the sake of material gain, and but this is a negative emotional response to the world around us. And we find the experience of living that kind of life is not fulfilling.

This is where the Caribbean is failing. The Caribbean people are not sufficiently politically educated. Even our great leaders left us a legacy that we can not even understand. The church has failed us as a society. Now we must start teaching people from their youth to live and be considerate for others. Life is not about me. It is what I can help my fellow human beings achieve. In that is my happiness and peace and joy.

Ebb and Flow

People in the Caribbean still believe that tourists are coming to take away something from the country. Tourism is who we are. We need to understand that. Those people need us to reach out to tourists, to embrace them and help them enjoy their vacation. They come to us seeking relaxation and fun. We must learn to construct our society to achieve this atmosphere.

Yet I do not see the Caribbean totally united in my lifetime. There is no sign of this happening soon. I cannot see the region having a common passport for all Caribbean countries. These countries are minutes away from each other, and each has its own prime minister. We are not prepared to make any sacrifice—our leaders are not—for the benefit of the peoples of the region.

The present politicians cannot accept defeat, even in the democratic atmosphere that prevails. It is hard for them to be statesman-like.

The Caribbean is blessed, even with the weather. With sound planning, the entire region can be self-sufficient in food and all basic necessities. Instead, most countries import everything, even basic food. Local businesses suffer because of this political mess.

The region needs men and women with leadership vision and foresight. Yet, such people cannot survive because the politicians fight and weed out the people who really can make a contribution. I can make a contribution, but the fight against me is frustrating. The whole system frustrates people.

Here in Canada, people measure you by your capability, not like in the Caribbean where you are measured by how useful you can be for the moment and then dumped as useless.

In a country like Canada, you can accomplish almost anything if health permits. Here no one looks down upon you. Here you can have a dream and the opportunities are there to achieve your dreams. A Saint Lucian national, Derek Walcott, became a successful writer, achieving a lot internationally. He won the Nobel Prize for Literature. But he did this outside the Caribbean. All great Caribbean people achieved their success overseas.

The Caribbean does not have the social system and environment that nurture people to achieve greatness. I thought I was a success in Saint Lucia. But was I really successful? Did I make a lasting impact on the society? No. Many people who tried their best to impact the societies of the Caribbean for good have lost their businesses, family, and place in the national fabric.

Today, I employ my discipline and good work ethic and I manage my business with peace and a quiet joy in my heart. Yet a certain sadness clouds my days because I want to see my homeland grow up and mature.

Concluding Advice

I grew up as a carefree boy on the sandy shores of the Caribbean Sea in Saint Lucia, in that romantic little village, Anse La Raye. I grew up and strived to lead my nation into becoming a solid twenty-first-century society. I saw my five children born and grow up there.

But the path I chose—to put my faith in the future of the Caribbean, to believe in that dream that beckoned me as a boy when I looked out at the world beyond the vastness of the blue sea covered by the blue sunny sky—that longing deep in my heart to build roots in that land collapsed within twenty-five years, like a sand castle on the beach.

I joined the emigration queue and boarded a plane to North America, something every ambitious Caribbean national does. The distant horizon did not bring my dream to me. Instead, it beckoned me away from Anse La Raye, to now live the twilight of my days in Toronto's snow-white suburbs.

My life experience has taught me the realities of the Caribbean emigrant culture. And we seem powerless under its onslaught. But I grew. I failed. I learned. Only that kind of intense personal experience teaches people. There is a message in my life. And I want the future generation—my grandchildren—to look at me and learn about life. The pain of loss is necessary to arrive at wisdom.

I was the first Saint Lucian to own a life insurance company. But I did not have the experience to keep what I had achieved. I squandered it all on friends and politics. And in a new nation, there is hardly any way to follow a trail, to look at a person's history and learn. We make our own history, because we are a young society, a growing nation. I have made that history. And I have learned valuable lessons. And I want to share those lessons with those who are going to walk in the path I have walked, who are going to step into my footprints.

I could have done more. But now in my twilight years, I have no desire to go back and correct those mistakes that I have made. That is for a new generation of younger people. Now, I live as a humble man. I spend my days in deep contemplation, no longer going after material things. I just want to help to educate and share knowledge with many people so that they do not make the mistakes that I made.

My years were not lost, because I have acquired and gained so much understanding, wisdom, and knowledge. You have to have deep strength inside you to absorb the pain that life in this world throws at you and get up and go again when you fall. That ability is bigger than if you had all the wealth in the world. In fact, today I am stronger because of my falls in life. I walk Toronto today with this storehouse of life experience embedded in my soul. And I live to share what I have learned.

That is my great legacy.

My fervent aspiration is that my life story will inspire and motivate the next generation to dream big and to step out with courage to achieve those dreams. My life experience taught me that nothing worthwhile in this life is attained free of sacrifice.

chapter twenty-two

REFLECTING ON MY LIFE LESSONS

"When one door closes, another opens; but we often look so long and so regretfully upon the closed door that we do not see the one that has opened for us." —Alexander Graham Bell

In documenting my life story in this book, I have sought to encourage and inspire and motivate you, the reader, with the story of the ebb and flow of my life experiences.

Human beings face all sorts of odds in just surviving day to day. To add to this journey of mere survival, the extra effort to build a noble life, to achieve above and beyond one's means, brings on added challenges.

Despite my journey of rising and falling, of ebbing and flowing, today I stand a contented and peaceful man. My heart rests assured that I have lived this life to the best of my ability. I have run the race, and at the end of my journey, I have one simple message for the world and for future generations.

Despite all the wealth and fame and power a man can achieve, at the end of the day what matters most is the state of his soul. What matters more than anything else is his faith in his Creator. What matters is building a relationship with our Lord. Everything else is vanity.

I am most thankful for the tremendous peace, love, and joy in my heart when I wake up in the morning. I hold no malice for any man, although I regret a few things that have transpired in my life. I am contented. I am peaceful. I look back on my life and see it well-lived. For that, I am eternally grateful. I have been fortunate and blessed beyond my wildest dream.

In fact, I do regret three events in my professional life. I should have supported Senator Rick Wayne of the Saint Lucia senate during the St. Helen Air debates in the house back in the 1990s when I was a senator. I regret not supporting him, because I discovered that he was right, and my decision to support the government was really out of blind loyalty to the prime minister, Mr. Kenny Anthony.

I also regret the fact that I apologized to former Prime Minister Vaughn Lewis for what he claims were some uncomplimentary remarks I made about him on radio and TV. He refused to address the Hotel and Tourism Association, of which I was the head at the time. However, because of the high level of confidence and respect I had for the chairman of the Tourist Board, Mr. Stephen McNamarra, and Mr. Cletus Springer, the permanent secretary in the Ministry of Tourism, and also the executive vice-president of the Saint Lucia Hotel and Tourism Association, Mr. Hillary Modeste, I apologized publicly to Mr. Lewis. I should not have done so. He addressed the association after I apologized, but I should have maintained my stance.

Something else I tend to regret is the fact that I once placed enormous confidence and trust and love in an aspiring political leader, Kenny Anthony, who became prime minister of Saint Lucia, with myself acting as chairman of the party that won the government, the Saint Lucia Labour Party. I assisted Anthony when he was down and out. I had met him in England and, being impressed with him then, urged him to make an effort to lead our country. I promised him I would work alongside him if he took the leadership of the party. I regret that, because I paid such a terrible sacrifice in my business and my life in Saint Lucia to support him and the party.

Up to this day, Mr. Anthony has not once personally expressed his thoughts on the demise of my extensive business holdings in Saint Lucia. I once thought I was his friend, but upon learning that he tacitly supported the seizure of my hotel by the state bank, I cannot feel anything but sadness and regret at having assisted him the way I once did.

However, having emigrated to Canada and being able to settle and follow the first-world lifestyle, I now understand that my life is about living with faith, trusting in the Creator for my peace and inner joy, and embracing the loving hands of family and loyal friends. My failures and successes, my life story, I realize, serve to strengthen and build my faith. I thus resolve to continue responding to the daily challenges of this life, but with this wisdom that comes from reflecting upon my walk through this world, I know it's all about my relationship with the Lord, who has been ever faithful to me.

For those times of trial, those betrayals of friendships, those days of challenges and struggles, we must remember what our Lord Jesus Christ went through. Life on this earth is not easy. He went through so much for us on the

Reflecting on My Life Lessons

cross. I have learned that developing spiritual faith is the most important goal of this life—like Abraham did, who even was willing to sacrifice his beloved son based on his faith.

We see Noah building an ark even when the rest of the world laughed at him and there was not one single sign of a flood coming. He, like Abraham, lived by faith and was rewarded. We must become men of faith, people of a spiritual foundation. These were men of faith, like Joseph, who went through so much in the Biblical account but came out ruling Egypt.

Thinking on these things, I have learned to live for forgiveness, to forgive the betrayals, to exhibit love. And I believe I am a better person for it. Living for faith, love, and forgiveness is the way to go. That's what I learned in my life's journey. Living this way, I guarantee you, leads to peace, joy, contentment, and the true love of souls who can be trusted.

Through the ebb and flow of my life, the solid rock I stand on is faith, love, and forgiveness.

part two

MY VISION FOR SOCIETY'S DEVELOPMENT

chapter twenty-three

INAUGURAL SPEECH

In the following speech, I laid out a vision for the cooperation of the tourism and agriculture sectors; for the two to join forces so that Saint Lucia could see broad-based development across economic sectors.

Political Leader, first deputy Political Leader, second deputy Political Leader, our esteemed guest speaker, members of the diplomatic corps, members of the Saint Lucia Labour Party's executive committee and national council, specially invited guests, well-wishers, brothers and sisters, ladies and gentlemen.

Brothers and sisters, I have a confession to make to you today. I must tell you how happy and proud I am today. It is an overpowering feeling. It is a good feeling, a very good feeling.

Let me, first of all, thank the political leader and the other members of the Executive Committee and national council for giving me the opportunity to serve, first as a vice-chairman and then as acting chairman of the party. I also wish to thank everyone who supported the party in the period leading up to and during the elections. It was, indeed, a pleasure for me to serve, especially during the election period, and I look forward to serving in whatever future capacity the party decides.

Brother and sisters, it feels good seeing the faces of so many of you who heard and heeded the clarion call that went out nearly eighteen months ago today. You heard the call that the redeemer had arrived who would take our party out of its self-imposed wilderness, and it was you who repeated this call from the mountaintops and in the valleys. It was your commitment and dedication to the cause, on those long days and sleepless nights, when nothing else mattered but *victory*.

Ebb and Flow

Sisters and brothers, it was you who kept the faith in the star, when the dark clouds of doubt and despair would engulf it. You encouraged our people not to lose hope and to stay focused on the cause and on the star.

You can therefore understand why I feel the way I feel today. But while I feel good and proud about the way we worked to achieve that sensational and historic victory, I am even more excited about the future of our party, our government, and our country.

Brothers and sisters, friends, today marks a momentous occasion in the history of this great and enduring party. Today, we bask in the realization of a thirty-year dream: a dream punctuated with the ever-present scars of toil and struggle culminating in the fulfillment of that dream, as the Labour Party holds its annual conference under a government of the Saint Lucia Labour Party.

Today, then, is also about celebration! It is about the celebration of the record achievement in the history of Saint Lucian elections and politics, with the Saint Lucia Labour Party winning sixteen of the seventeen parliamentary seats; the celebration of a people who revolted against their marginalization, harassment, and victimization under the former regime. And, while we are at it, brothers and sisters, we must pay tribute to one of the founding fathers of the Saint Lucia Labour Party, and the first chief minister of Saint Lucia, the great and inimitable George F.L. Charles, after whom one of our airports is now named.

Brothers and sisters, today we gather here in the history-making constituency of Babonneau to chart a new course in the history of the beloved party. In charting this new course, we give recognition to the renewal of our friendships and the development of new ones. In charting this new course, we are cognizant that our new party structure must be strengthened in every aspect to reflect the dictates of a vibrant, fiercely competitive, and technologically based twenty-first century.

But brothers and sisters, we fought the election campaign as "Team Labour," and we must salute our hardworking team of cabinet ministers for the great job which they have done over the best part of five months. They have showed us clearly that they have the experience, the knowledge, and the commitment to manage their respective ministries. They have made us all very proud. We know that they will keep up the good work.

Brothers and sisters, there is a lot of work to be done by Team Labour. Results will not come overnight, and some may grow impatient. That would be very natural. But we must keep the faith. Brothers and sisters, we must hold our

Inaugural Speech

formation. We must not let down our guard, for while we have defeated the enemy, we must not assume that the enemy is dead.

In the months ahead, we will face our greatest challenge, that of completing the change from a party in opposition to a party in government. It is important that we adjust to this change, as this will give us the disciplined framework in which we can and must act.

In opposition, brothers and sisters, we had a goal, and we know clearly what we had to do to reach that goal. We know what resources were available. Most importantly, we know the forces we were up against. These things gave us the discipline and the formation, which we maintained throughout the election campaign.

In government, it is a little more difficult to identify a goal. The resources too are not easily identified, and even when it is identified, it is not easily made available, and it is not within our control. The enemy is now a disintegrated force. These things can make us complacent and carefree and undisciplined.

Today, after a succession of other leaders, the baton has been passed to another giant of a leader, in the person of Dr. Kenny D. Anthony. Saint Lucia Labour Party has found a leader who commands the respect, admiration, and love of persons from both sides of the political fence. It is, therefore, incumbent upon us to share in and support the vision of our leader while allowing him time to implement that vision.

In moving to a party in government, we will need to carry over some of the things that worked so well for us so far, while in opposition. In the same way we defended our party while in opposition, we must defend the actions of our government. When we do not understand the reasons why certain things are being done, we must seek explanation and clarification through branch meetings or executive meetings, or directly from the minister concerned.

Above all, brothers and sisters, we must learn to disagree with one another without being disagreeable. We must learn to exercise our democratic right to question and to challenge, but we must be prepared to yield in the face of superior logic or in the interest of the stability of the government. As chairman of this party, I have defended and will continue to defend the right of any member of our party to question and challenge from within, in keeping with the procedures laid down. I will not, however, encourage those who prefer to challenge and question outside of the procedures laid down in our constitution.

Brothers and sisters, there is a very exciting period before us as we approach the twenty-first century. But today isn't just about history. It is also about modernization, communication, education, innovation, participation, and the fostering and strengthening of meaningful relationships. Our party cannot afford to stand still amidst lightning-fast global changes, because to stand still is to die.

So we must reflect a modernized outlook. We are living in the information age, where the volume and speed of information transmission is staggering. Gone is the complexity associated with information technology in the past; today, the Labour Party is on the Internet! In addressing the modernization issue, therefore, we must seek ways and means of harnessing the enormous power of information technology.

The Labour Party must utilize and seek to recruit existing skills to define, collect, manipulate, and analyze data and disseminate information inside and outside of the party for maximum effect. We must also ensure that these various items of information reach our intended audiences at the right time! Information is power, but disseminating that information when it is already in the public domain is like letting your opponents see your cards in a poker game, as this leaves you a seriously weakened position.

Our secretariat must and will become the party's communication hub, whether it be written or oral, between the party and government, between the secretariat and the outside world. We must be well-structured and coherent. Communication must not be left to chance. A message could become lost in several ways; there must be follow-up and a genuine attempt to determine whether the recipient of the message understood the gist of it.

The value of political education cannot be overemphasized. Education is the key element in the developmental thrust of this party. We must, however, avoid indoctrination and concentrate solely on education indoctrination, with all that that signifies. This is the major reason why many of our people cannot adequately address significant national issues beyond the narrow realm of party politics.

We must, and will, begin the process of broad-based political education—a political education that must be rooted in objectivity. This education must be aimed at *all* our people through public debate and discussion, lectures, newspaper articles, and pamphlets. The idea is to stimulate individual and collective thinking to look at issues or arguments based on their merit, rather than through a looking-glass tainted with political dogma.

However, we must re-educate ourselves first before we begin to educate others! In that regard, therefore, our attitudes—particularly with respect to

Inaugural Speech

criticism—must change; our leadership roles must be taken seriously. Our various responsibilities must be taken seriously, and we must become universal in our outlook. Our party and our government must take the lead in this Herculean but vitally important task. I firmly believe that we'll be applauded for it in the years to come.

In all of this, innovation plays a critical role. Life and its myriad subtleties is all about evolution. We must shape our political education through innovation. To do so, we shall build upon some of the old ways and introduce fresh, insightful methods. Innovation isn't necessarily about being first in the introduction of a new idea, but it is about being successful in the implementation of it. We must, therefore, invest in research. Our ability to forge ahead and stay ahead of the pack depends on it.

Our party would not be the same without the alliances or relationships, which we have fashioned over the years with other organizations. We are in a position now to make those relationships work even better, to seek new, meaningful alliances, which will rebound to the benefit of the party. We must not be afraid, hesitant, or half-hearted about fostering those relationships if they appear healthy and progressive.

In seeking new alliances, we must actively target local mothers' and fathers' groups, sports and cultural clubs, social and/or voluntary organizations, business groupings, and any other lawful organization or group with which we can form a working relationship or common bond. We must also continue the process of establishing regional and international branches or chapters of the party. The dynamic, people-oriented nature of our mission makes it mandatory that we do so.

The relationship between the party and the government is still a vague area, which is in the discussion stage. What must be stressed, however, is that the Saint Lucia Labour Party must protect the Saint Lucia Labour Party government. However, we cannot, and will not, buy into the idea that the party is just an instrument used to catapult politicians into power every five years.

All of this must not be effected in a vacuum. The theme running through all our endeavours is people. Mechanisms must be instituted to allow the effective participation of our members in processes of the party. Our leadership must not insulate itself behind a barrier of isolation and issue directives therefrom.

Members must be made to feel part of the consultation process. This process will guarantee the free flow of information from the rank-and-file to the leadership and vice-versa. Communication is a two-way street along which we must all walk.

Ebb and Flow

The alienation of our members through non-participation is dangerous. Alienation drives our members into the street, and elsewhere, to engage in practices harmful to our organization. We must heed the lessons of the past and listen to our members more often. So participation is paramount. Through participation, the chances are greater that we'll achieve consensus and we know that consensus promotes democracy. Democracy is about people!

Equally important is the recognition that must be given to the fact that many of our members were denied equal opportunity on the basis of their political affiliation under the former regime. We must begin to address this situation now. I am not advocating that we effect the same discriminatory practices used by the former government; that is counter-productive and not in keeping with the new vision of the Labour Party. But we must introduce a mechanism to ensure that those persons who felt the brunt of UWP anti-labour behaviour in the past get a chance under this Labour Party government to have a fair share of the economic cake.

It is imperative, therefore, at this conference, that we make the right decisions. It is imperative that we set the stage for our successful entry into the politics of the future. This occasion must not be one for empty rhetoric and breast-beating but must reflect our ability to set standards and project into the future.

What we do here today must be monitored and evaluated over the next year. The right sensors must be established so that corrective mechanisms can quickly kick in when they need to. Today, then, is the first day in the life of the party. What we do here today will determine the quality of life of the party for the rest of that life!

As we ponder the twenty-first century with all its uncertainties and opportunities, we know that there are numerous challenges waiting to be met: some of them old, most of them new. I have every confidence that we shall meet those challenges and triumph!

It is with great pride and pleasure, therefore, that I welcome you, all of you, to this: the 1997 Conference of Delegates of the Saint Lucia Labour Party.

chapter twenty-four

TOURISM ASSOCIATION SPEECH

I made the following speech against the background of the need for a visionary strategy for Saint Lucia's economically important tourism industry.

In this speech I explain the need for a new direction for the national tourism industry, because I was the outgoing president of the association. The tourism industry is close to my heart, and as a hotelier myself, I wanted to direct the industry into a sustainable and more vibrant economic pillar of the country's economic tripod.

Saint Lucia Hotel and Tourism Association (SLHTA)—37th Annual General Meeting, Held on Friday, December 3, 1999, at Club Med, Under the Theme *Tourism 2000 and Beyond: Rising Confidently to Meet the Challenges of the Future* President's Report, Presented by Senator Noel N.S. Cadasse

This 37th Annual general Meeting of the Saint Lucia Hotel and Tourism Association (SLHTA) is taking place at a crucial juncture, which calls for decisive action and a proactive stance from all of us gathered here today, who must continue to play a pivotal role if this vitally important tourism industry is to help sustain our economy. I say crucial, because we are just about entering the twenty-first century, which will continue to pose tremendous possibilities and challenges to small island economies, such as our own economy that is grappling with horrendous external shocks from the impact of trade liberalization in particular and globalization in general. Therefore, as we prepare for those external shocks we must be reminded of the adage: "The survival of the fittest!"

Ladies and gentlemen, it is time for serious reflection and even introspection as we venture into the unknown; but nevertheless, "rising confidently to meet the challenges of the future" as far as tourism development is concerned.

Ebb and Flow

I say unknown, because as a small island state, Saint Lucia must struggle against the odds of globalization and vulnerability to both nature and manmade disaster. In the past, we have learned a great deal from the recalcitrant behaviour of workers and have also suffered the ravages of hurricanes and tropical storms, which have brought our economy to a grinding halt on a number of occasions. Indeed, we are completely powerless and vulnerable to those disasters.

Before I go any further, let me pause to express the empathy of our association and my own concern for those towns and communities which suffered at the hands of Lenny, specifically those in Gros Islet, Anse La Raye, Soufriere, and Canaries. Plus, the hotels, restaurants, and other beachfront properties which suffered structural damage and economic losses as a result of the sea surges brought on by Lenny. We trust that the recovery effort will be swift so that we can all be ready to receive guests for the upcoming winter season.

Over the last twelve months, the growth potential of tourism in Saint Lucia has been very much in evidence. There has been a virtual boom in hotel developments and expansions, and information received from the ministries of Tourism and Planning suggest that this upsurge in construction will continue well into the next two to three years. We must ask ourselves whether the tourism sector in particular and the entire society in general is ready for this growth. Are we as the umbrella private sector organization in the industry preparing that industry for the challenges of absorbing and sustaining that growth?

This is a question that I hope that all of us are asking ourselves, because these adjustments required have to be made at the level of individual companies, as well as at the level of the sub sectors and by our association itself. We will also want to ask the question "Is the government doing enough?"

As I reflect quickly on certain developments during the last year, I hope to create a platform for outlining some of the key challenges that I see ahead for tourism in Saint Lucia.

Education and Awareness

I believe that the greatest benefit that our association can provide to our members and to the industry as a whole is through education. Indeed this is one of the primary reasons why our general meetings are structured in the manner that they are. We must pursue our educational drive at all possible levels.

The association must accept the challenge thrown out by the minister on the last occasion at which he addressed us, and which I emphasized at our last

Tourism Association Speech

quarterly general meeting, to educate the wider community on the basic functioning and benefits of the tourism industry. We must place more emphasis on the continuous education and sensitization of our employees in all quarters of the industry. This is a challenge for the broader membership, not just hotels. And we must not be afraid to face the challenge at even the most rudimentary level, including basic literacy training.

This is a cause that I hold dearly. As we are drawn into the new millennium, with much of the future of the industry being driven by the developments in technology, we must strengthen our resolve to eradicate illiteracy in this country.

Many of our members are often faced with the constraint of coping with employees that are at best semi-literate. We applaud the recent initiative of the government to refocus some of its resources towards the expansion of its adult literacy program. Some of our members are already taking initiative in-house to deal with the problem. We must spare no effort in ensuring that this scourge is totally eradicated within the shortest possible time, and I challenge the government and the private sector to devise appropriate approaches to tackle this problem on a collaborative and complementary basis.

For its own part, the association continues to support our members in providing a sound basic education to their children through the annual award of bursaries for those who have been successful in their Common Entrance examinations. The association is currently supporting twenty bursary holders each at a level of $750 annually, amounting to a sum total contribution of $15,000 per year towards secondary education. These awards are financed out of the proceeds of the annual Miss SLHTA Pageant.

It is now time for us to reach out more to the schools, particularly at the primary and secondary levels. There is scope for introducing a lecture or industry career talk series targeting these levels of education system. There is also a need to produce appropriate textbooks and teaching aids to assist teachers in more effectively delivering tourism education as part of the school curriculum. These are initiatives that easily lend themselves to public/private sector collaboration.

We must commit ourselves to actively pursue these projects if the school children of today are to become the next generation of service industry employees.

Human Resource Development

As the growth of the industry is spurred on by the new investments in hotel plant and air and sea port infrastructure and by the parallel growth in visitor arrivals, perhaps the greatest challenge which this poses to both the private sector and the government is to prepare Saint Lucians to take up the many employment opportunities which this growth creates.

There is a dire need now to expand the availability and scope of training opportunities for both entry level workers in the industry and for the upgrading of the skills and knowledge base of persons already employed in the industry. In addressing that need, nationals must be enabled to carve out distinct career paths and opportunities for themselves, which lead them right to the very top levels of management.

Having said this, I want to publicly recognize the achievements of the Saint Lucians within our midst who through their hard work and selfless commitment have assumed the reins of top management within the hotel sector—Mr. Lawrence Samuel, General Manager of Windjammer Landing Villa Beach Resort, Mr. Marc Jonvill of Sandals La Toc, Ms. Berthia Parle, General Manager of Bay Gardens, and most recently, Ms. Gilda Samuel, General Manager of Glencastle Resort, and Mr. Edmund Sidonie, General Manager of the Rex Papillion. These individuals have paved the way and set the benchmark for fellow Saint Lucians in the industry to aspire to in the new millennium.

At the entry level, we need to create the environment and put in place the necessary incentives to motivate and attract the youth to deliberately seek out a livelihood in the industry as their first choice of employment. And once that opportunity is afforded them, these young persons must ensure that they approach their jobs with pride and dignity. At the same time, they must be encouraged and justly rewarded by their employers for providing the level of quality service that will ensure that our tourism product remains competitive and that our companies remain viable.

The honourable prime minister recently announced the government's intention to earmark a factory shell in the north of the island for the conduct of short-term, on-demand preparatory skills training for the service sector (among other sectors) catering to school leavers who do not possess the minimum requirements to pursue further education.

This is a most welcome initiative, given the insufficient capacity of the island's comprehensive schools to meet all national demands for job and technical skills training. The tourism industry can stand to benefit significantly from this new thrust, not only from the training of students in various hotel trades, but also from the upgrading of skills in other technical trades such as plumbing, computer systems maintenance, electrical engineering, landscaping architecture, interior decorating, mechanical engineering—just to name a few. These skills are currently in short supply in the tourism industry.

The association has been actively involved in assisting with the process of planning the design of the proposed Hospitality Training Institute earmarked for the Massade area, which is to be operated by the Sir Arthur Lewis Community College. In the interim we have, certainly in the food and beverage area, offered to assist the college in the delivery of their program. There are opportunities to further this collaboration in a more comprehensive and systematic way, and the association challenges hospitality professions, as well as our hotel and restaurant members to provide some voluntary support and to assist with additional apprenticeship programs, to complement the efforts of the community college.

The association will seek to maximize short-term training opportunities available under the recently launched Caribbean Regional HRD Program for Economic Competitiveness (CPEC), which is based in Saint Lucia and funded by the Canadian government. We have been in discussion with the local management team and are currently preparing a proposal for short-term training, jointly with the Ministry of Tourism. The Caribbean Hotel Association has also applied for a grant under the project to finance a program of "on property" technical assistance to the small hotel sector, to complement the OAS Small Hotels Project. This will cover a variety of areas, including front office, table service, housekeeping, basic interior decorating, budgeting, etc. We will of course continue to pursue new short-term opportunities through the CHA. We intend to place particular emphasis on customer-service training, as this seems to be the area of greatest demand within the membership.

In terms of long-term training opportunities, the association will continue to work with the Mount Saint Vincent University in Canada to maximize the opportunities available to staff in the industry to pursue higher education certification, using the very affordable approach of distance learning. The SLHTA is currently facilitating a scholarship program in which seven industry employees are enrolled to read for a bachelor's degree in Tourism and Hospitality Management at that university. This is a collaborative effort with the Ministry of Human Resource Development. We are jointly exploring with the government the possibility of expanding this scholarship program to take in a second batch of students. SLHTA members will also continue to benefit from annual scholarships available from the Caribbean Hotel Foundation.

The human resource development demands and opportunities of the industry are many and varied, and the time has most certainly come for employers and the government to collaborate much more closely in the preparation and financing of a comprehensive human resource development plan for the tourism industry. The absence of such a plan at this point in time surely should not prevent us from continuing to pursue training initiatives that are already in the pipeline, but we need to determine with urgency the full range of training and human development needs of the industry, identify new innovative strategies, and invest the necessary resources in the preparation of the people whose tireless efforts make the industry work. The current approach of training is much too ad hoc; it tends to be reactive and externally propelled and is devoid of a strategic basis.

One of the new strategies I would like to propose to the government at this juncture is to offer tax credits to companies in the industry who provide certified short-term training to their staff at recognized regional and international professional institutes. This suggestion might be considered within the framework of a set of critical target areas to be agreed with the government. The benefits of this approach would be twofold. This would encourage companies to invest substantially more resources in training needs and opportunities, since the training choices would be driven by the private sector, which has the expert knowledge of the best available opportunities. I would wish the government to consider working with the association to develop this proposal for possible inclusion in its first budget for the new millennium.

Crime and Harassment

It never goes away. The tourism industry is under the constant threat of crime and harassment. And the more growth we experience, the greater the probability that one of our guests is likely to become a victim of this scourge. We must never let down our guard nor must we ever lose our resolve to eradicate this menace, which continually threatens to undermine the industry.

The police department has reported a reduced level of crime against visitors for the last few months compared to last year. I wish to commend the police for their efforts and improved performance. However, while we would all be happy to believe that this apparent reduction in the incidence of crime will be a new trend, we are cautiously optimistic for a number of reasons. Firstly, many of our hoteliers have lost faith that the police will take any decisive action when crimes are reported; as a result, many incidents are not reported.

Secondly, while there has been some improvement in the establishment of police patrols in some heavily trafficked tourist areas, there is a blatant display of disinterest by many police officers in intervening in situations in which visitors are under threat of harassment or abuse. Clearly these police officers need to adopt a much more proactive, interactive, and preventative approach to dealing with situations that have the potential to lead to some type of disorderly behaviour or escalate into criminal activity. Our citizens as well as our guests need to feel a sense that they are being protected.

Thirdly, when crimes are reported, the procedure for filing the report is so longwinded that the opportunity to seek redress during the duration of the stay of the visitor is often lost. This is compounded by the slow pace of the processing of the cases in the judicial system. It is interesting and welcoming that the government is contemplating the establishment of a tribunal to deal with industrial relations issues. The tourism industry has been calling for a long time now for a separate court structure to deal with crime against visitors. This too must be considered as an integral part of government's program to reform the judicial system.

At the same time, the association has moved to strengthen and consolidate its internal arrangements for security of guests and property by reconstituting our Board Committee on Crime and Security under the able leadership of Mr. Cuthbert Phillips, a former commissioner of police. That committee has redesigned the format for reporting of cases of crime and harassment so that the industry can get a better handle on the true extent of these cases, to identify the problem areas, and to work more closely with the police in taking the necessary remedial action.

Preservation of the Environment

The physical environment has come under much scrutiny over the last few months primarily as a result of attempts to increase awareness of the population of the problem of solid waste management, which, incidentally, becomes particularly acute after the sort of storm activity that Saint Lucia experienced recently.

We applaud the efforts of the Saint Lucia Heritage Tourism Project in trying to raise community awareness, the Solid Waste Management Authority in introducing new systems and guidelines to better manage the problem, and the National Conservation Authority and the Saint Lucia National Trust for their ongoing clean-up efforts. However, caring for the environment means much more than cleaning up the road verges in Castries and in other regions, or beach clean-ups, much as these activities are commendable and welcome.

These efforts must be complemented by an educational drive targeting in particular the persons who inhabit communities in the upper reaches and along the island's watersheds, who undertake domestic and agricultural and other economic activities in these areas. The problems of pollution of some of our bays do not start with the activities that are located nearest to them, many of which are tourism related. But it is the coastal environment that suffers the accumulated negative impacts.

This is a potentially serious problem, which must be addressed in a timely manner if the tourism industry is to be protected from the hazard of pollution of our coastal waters, on which the industry so vitally depends. This is an environmental threat looming on the horizon of Saint Lucia's tourism, which we cannot afford to ignore as we seek to re-emphasize our international image as a clean and naturally beautiful destination.

We commend the Solid Waste Management Authority for moving to establish a national policy and legislative framework on the management of solid as well as liquid waste. This type of legislation, together with a comprehensive regime for the management of land use in the island's precious watershed, needs to be introduced and strictly enforced with the greatest urgency. Voluntary efforts and education and awareness building are essential elements of the foundation for ensuring a cleaner and healthier environment, but basic human nature also demands the enactment of tough legislation to force the discipline and social responsibility on persons who refuse to see any further than their own selfish gain.

Effective Marketing

We have been blessed in many ways with the natural assets that support the comparative advantage which tourism enjoys as an economic activity in the islands of the Caribbean. But that comparative advantage can only be mobilized to our full benefit if we protect these assets and effectively market the natural virtues of our tourism product. And these include the warmth, generosity, hospitality, and friendliness of Saint Lucians, as well as the stunning natural beauty of the island.

In this regard, I believe that on the public sector side, the Saint Lucia Heritage Tourism Program is particularly well placed to give a much-needed boost to the overall marketing effort of the destination. In the private sector, we recognize the tremendous contribution that the large hotels already make to the marketing thrust of the destination by virtue of the large amount that they continue to spend on the marketing of their properties.

I want to challenge the entire sector to give more prominence to our small hotels in the destination's new marketing thrust, with their friendly intimacy

Tourism Association Speech

and homely character. We at the association are following closely the progress of the OAS-funded Small Hotels Project, which will seek to create a more easily marketable identity for the small hotel product, as well as assist in sourcing low-cost financing for much-needed product improvements.

The traditional distribution channels for marketing programs will continue to feature prominently in our development plans; however we need to give the global travel community more compelling reasons to visit Saint Lucia and thereby lay the basis for long-term growth of visitor arrivals. This can only be achieved if more resources are put into a new marketing thrust to support the renewed image for Saint Lucia, which the tourist board is seeking to create under the repositioning strategy for the destination.

We recognize the need for government to allocate a substantial proportion of its current resources directly towards programs for social betterment. However, there is an equally, if not more urgent, need to invest in the income-generating capacity of the productive sectors of the economy, which can in turn be used to support the government's social program. Tourism marketing must be regarded as one such area of investment, and a firm decision has to be taken by the government to provide the tourist board with the resources that it requires to consolidate and expand our activities and presence in the tourism markets that produce the lifeblood of the tourism business.

Air Access

The adequacy of airlift from the major source markets for our tourism destination continues to be an issue of great strategic importance to the industry and one over which we seem to be able to exercise very little influence. This is why the commercially aggressive initiatives taken by regional airlines such as Jamaica and BWIA are so welcome and so well-received and why the plight of LIAT and Helen Air is of such great concern to the industry.

The association throws out the challenge to our members to continue to support these regional airlines in their commercial endeavours and to the government to continue to exercise prudence and good judgment in coming to their assistance and in establishing mutually beneficial partnerships where such opportunities present themselves.

Beyond the commercial growth prospects being exploited by the regional airlines, the government itself, in collaboration with the tourism private sector, must continuously search out the most cost-effective opportunities for bringing in additional airline seats into Saint Lucia. This is particularly critical during this period of boom in hotel room construction, which is creating the level of demand that will justify additional direct air services. A more systematic, proactive, and planned approach must be adopted to negotiations with new potential carriers, particularly those that seem to be operating viably in neighbouring islands, as well as charter companies, which can add Saint Lucia as a destination on their itinerary.

As well, there must be closer collaboration and an integration of the processes of decision making within the Air Licensing Authority, the Air Services Committee, the Saint Lucia Tourist Board, the Saint Lucia Air and Sea Ports Authority, and the Saint Lucia Hotel and Tourism Association in relation to new airline services.

The association is heartened to learn that the tourist board has come to an arrangement with Condor Airlines that will allow for continuation of the services into Saint Lucia for this coming winter season and year round. We trust that the consolidation of that partnership marks the beginning of a revitalized marketing effort to secure an increased level of visitation from the German market. Both our large and small hotel properties are keen to exploit the growth prospects in that market.

Development of the Product

When we speak of the new millennium, we tend to contemplate the uncertainties, the challenges, and the opportunities that the future will pose. But in large measure, we really should be focusing on moving quickly and decisively to attempt to catch up with the realities of the present.

This is the scenario that we face when we think of the state of development of some aspects of our tourism product. In many respects we are lagging behind. And in saying so, I think of the underdevelopment of sports tourism, the quality of our entertainment, the quality of health services, our level of customer service, the congestion at Hewannorra Airport on a Sunday, and indeed the absence of gaming facilities. As a destination, we need to invest more in the establishment of sporting facilities. There are opportunities for generating increased visitation to Saint Lucia through the development of sport such as cricket—a national stadium of international standard is badly needed.

The quality of musical entertainment in Saint Lucia leaves much room for improvement. We commend the efforts of the government in attempting to assist musicians to improve their level of organization, professionalism, and their business prospects in general. The SLHTA is represented on that working group. I want to throw out the challenge to the hotel sector in particular to give

Tourism Association Speech

more support to the local music industry by featuring more local artists at hotel entertainment functions. The tourism industry constitutes a significant component of the market for local entertainers, and it is hoped that as the quality of that entertainment product improves, the ability of entertainers to command more attractive returns would increase in tandem.

Our health services infrastructure is in dire need of upgrading. In that regard, we welcome the announcement by the government of plans to construct a new hospital. Apart from the long overdue improvement in health service to the general public, this should allow the destination to position itself more favourably to gain the confidence and attract a larger share of the growing market for travel by the elderly in particular, who need the assurance of the availability of modern, efficient, and reliable health services.

The Sunday congestion and bustle at Hewannorra Airport can only get worse with the increased number of international flights which the growth of the industry is going to attract over the next two to three years. Action has to be taken now to alleviate the current situation and to plan ahead for an upgraded level of passenger service, including customs and immigration clearance, luggage conveyance, as well as the quality of taxi services.

We are aware that the local taxi association and the government are making a concerted effort to improve the standard of tourism transportation. However the association will not pretend that all is well. We continue to receive complaints about the aggressive attitude of taxi drivers. This does not augur well for the first impression that the visitor gets on arrival into Saint Lucia. Let me say a quick word to our drivers that no amount of training, legislation, or concessions will make you the sort of model driver that the industry needs. It is your own acceptance of the responsibility to be professional, courteous, and disciplined that will make the difference.

The association is committed to supporting your growth and development as evidenced through our endorsement of your exclusive agreement with the ground handlers' sector. We must let you know, however, that the overwhelming sentiment is for the taxi sector to continue to grow and develop to the stage that the market for tourism transportation will be self regulating, such that only those drivers who provide the required level of quality service will be given the opportunity to do so.

Tourism is an internationally liberalized and highly competitive industry. Our tourism economy cannot afford to continue to accommodate and subsidize substandard service and increasing taxi fares. Self-regulation, quality, and efficiency improvements and open price competition are the order of the day. This is the accepted norm in all industries and sectors—bananas, water services, telecommunications, to name a few. The taxi sector should be no exception. The importance to the overall visitor experience of improving the quality and competitiveness of the vital service that you provide cannot be overemphasized.

There are many more aspects of the tourism product that are in need of greater focus, but before I leave the subject, I must touch on one area which has generated some debate, and that is the issue of gaming. I believe that the reservations regarding the possible ill effects of casinos are overblown.

The idea is a novel one for Saint Lucia, and as with any other novel idea, public opinion tends to weigh in the direction of resisting change. Casinos operate profitably and with strict regulations in many other destinations in the Caribbean. Indeed our guest speaker today hails from the Bahamas, where gaming has been responsibly and successfully interwoven into the fabric of the total tourism product. Indeed, the establishment of resorts with gaming facilities contributed significantly to the recovery and growth of tourism in the Bahamas.

Saint Lucia's tourism is currently riding on a wave of growth, and the introduction of gaming at this time can only enhance our growth opportunities and enrich our product mix. Put very plainly, the perspective that the industry adopts on the introduction of gaming in Saint Lucia is that it is an amenity of wide international appeal that provides the visitor with an additional form of entertainment and recreation. The rationale underlying the introduction of gaming must be the wider benefits which it offers, not only in terms of visitor enjoyment, employment, incomes, and government revenues, but also in terms of the additional investment which a government can leverage by offering a gaming license to a reputable operator. Once the relevant legislation is passed, the government has the opportunity to utilize that prerogative in a strategic and judicious manner, to maximize the level of investment and overall economic benefit, which resorts will inject into the destination as a condition for operating a casino.

Collaboration with the Public Sector

Many of the challenges and imperatives on which I have spoken today require as a basic necessity the establishment of a close working relationship with the government and the broader public sector. The association had made this point on many occasions, and takes this opportunity in the presence of the honourable prime minister, Dr. Kenny Anthony, to repeat that call for closer public-private sector collaboration. There will always be some differences of

Tourism Association Speech

perspective on certain issues and problems affecting the industry. But we cannot afford not to establish a permanent mechanism to facilitate discussion of priority concerns as well as opportunities for sustaining and better managing the growth of the industry.

We should not enter the new millennium simply talking about the need to work closer together. We must simply make it happen. Some of the strategic decisions that need to be taken to move the industry forward really cannot be taken by either the government or the private sector on their own. Until we firmly commit ourselves to working together to achieve a set of common objectives, tourism industry partners will never be able to optimize the benefits of the growth of the industry. The association has recognized the need to work with the government on many initiatives existing and proposed. I sincerely trust that the government feels likewise.

I want to applaud the recent initiative taken by the government to establish an inter-ministerial committee on tourism. We are encouraged by this cross-sector approach to dealing with the priority needs of the tourism industry form the government's perspective. We see the potential for this inter-ministerial mechanism to evolve into an interface with the private sector on a broad range of issues and developments that affect the tourism industry. I use this opportunity today to put that proposal forward to the government for its early consideration.

As an industry grows, it becomes increasingly important to support the association that represents the private sector concerns of that industry. In so doing, members must not succumb to the temptation to ask, "What is the association doing for my business?" Rather, members should challenge the association to provide them with the representation and services they require to improve their prospects of operating more viably.

The first step in this process is to recognize that we all have the responsibility to inform the association of our needs so that the association can be put in a position to respond accordingly. We cannot have the answers if we do not know what the questions are.

The association itself is seeking to become more proactive and dynamic in its mode of operation so that it can anticipate threats to and opportunities for the industry and take the appropriate actions or adopt strategic positions that service the collective interests of members.

Members must be warned not to be passive witnesses to the rapid pace of growth and development of the tourism industry. The challenge that is thrown out to all of us is to equip ourselves to be part of the process and not wait until development mushrooms around us to ask, "What is the government doing for us?" or "What is the association doing to protect our interests?"

We will not relinquish our responsibility to lobby and advocate for change that will benefit the industry, nor will we shy away from speaking out against developments which could adversely affect tourism. Even in such instances, we need to have information and the views of our members to support our case.

I therefore want to urge members to be more forthcoming with their concerns and to rally around the association when we seek to provide representation on an issue of common interest.

Finally, each member must accept the individual responsibility to contribute to the financial viability of the association. The association cannot continue to function without your voluntary financial input. This applies equally to the payment of annual dues as it does to membership support of fundraising activities and projects.

Membership support on both of these fronts has dwindled over this past year, and the tragedy of this situation is that it is happening at a time when the association will be required and called upon to be much more active in promoting the interest of members and in securing the future of the industry.

The future of the association is literally in your hands. The decision is yours to either let it go under or to join together to carry our association forward into the new millennium.

In closing, I want to thank the board of directors, the general membership, and Mrs. Ilene Paul of the secretariat. There are also a few persons in the tourism industry of whom I must make special mention in view of their moral support and repeated wise counselling to me personally. They are Berthia Parle, George Joosten, and Richard Michelin. I owe them a debt of gratitude!

At this point, it is with regret that I now formally announce my decision to step down as SLHTA president. Recent developments in my business and professional life have taken a serious toll on my family and myself. I need time to re-energize and to recuperate from mental and physical strain. The association's work requires a certain level of commitment, focus, and organization; such I cannot give at this present time.

However, I do believe there are others in our midst who are quite capable of taking the mantle of leadership of the SLHTA to the next critical stage of communal involvement and development. Rest assured, that you can count on me to continue to serve the association in an ordinary capacity.

Tourism Association Speech

I wish you all a very merry Christmas, God's blessings for the New Year, and a prosperous tourism season while we "Rise Confidently to Meet the Challenges of the Future."

chapter twenty-five

POLITICAL SPEECH, VIEUX FORT

In the following speech, I shared the motivation and challenge for a new government. I was called upon by the prime minister, Dr. Kenny Anthony—who was the then parliamentary representative of the Vieux Fort South constituency—to address his constituents.

The remarks made here are still relevant today.

Keeping Alive Grassroots Community Spirit
By Senator Noel N.S. Cadasse, guest speaker at the Vieux Fort South Constituency Group Annual Conference on Sunday September 26, 1999

Honourable Prime Minister, Party Leader, and Parliamentary Representative for Vieux Fort South, Dr. Kenny Anthony, other ministers of government, executive members of the Saint Lucia Labour Party (SLP), members of the SLP Vieux Fort South Constituency Group, other SLP members, supporters, well wishers, invited guests, ladies and gentlemen. *Bon apwe midi mamai Laba*!

I am greatly delighted and do feel honoured to be given this rare opportunity of being the guest speaker on the occasion of the annual conference of the Vieux Fort South Constituency Group, which happens to be the constituency of our esteemed prime minister and party leader, Dr. Kenny Anthony. Besides, it is particularly a joyous moment for me personally to address the constituents of what has become known as "The New Frontier," which promises to lay a solid economic base from which this country will confidently take up the many challenges of the twenty-first century and beyond.

Therefore, the role of this constituency group must be clearly defined in view of the overall objective of "Keeping Alive Grassroots Community Spirit."

Ebb and Flow

We want to simply nurture a spirit of love, togetherness, loyalty, commitment, and camaraderie. It is those very same principles that form the basis of good family life and togetherness. We pray together. We work together. We live engaged in positive and independent thinking.

However, we have seen a new political process and culture emerging in this country with the advent of a new SLP administration under the able leadership of Dr. Kenny Anthony, who has introduced a measure of change in the governance of this country. Yet that new political thrust and method of governance has been painful in some instances, causing some disquiet and alarm in certain quarters. Others have been severely critical of the changes taking place in the governance of the country, in a lame attempt to undermine the political process. Beware, my brothers and sisters, of those political detractors!

But on the economic front, we have seen some well-deserved changes now taking place around us. For example, the internet (information super highway) and the telecommunications industry have made it possible for us to communicate instantly throughout the world. And coming closer to home, look at the developments now taking place in Saint Lucia and in Vieux Fort in particular, which I am sure your parliamentary representative will further articulate. So let us not be afraid of change and support the collective leadership and wisdom of our government.

May I remind you that we are not merely working for our present generation but we are seeking to provide a sustainable environment for future generations to live, work, and play. This is where "the New Frontier" will assist in providing the economic, social, and cultural development needed to sustain our country and our people. It is for this reason that we must rally behind the government when it takes bold steps and seemingly unpopular decisions to prepare our country for the future and the new millennium.

In support of this expression, my brothers and sisters, I want to state categorically that I support the decision of the government to guarantee a loan for Helen Air Corporation in recent times.

As a constituency group, your responsibility is to ensure that we contribute to the development of our community and the society as a whole. We must not be caught in the petty political squabbles and infighting that very often undermine the political process. We must stand beside our party leader in his resolve to get the work done and to get it done promptly. We must also ignore and avoid the pettiness and greed permeating our community like wild fire. We must stand up against petty jealousies, which sometimes lead to self-destruction.

Political Speech, Vieux Fort

The government was perceived in the past as a saviour of all things and all persons. This perception, unfortunately, has led to an over-reliance on political favours, which could not be realistically delivered, and as a consequence, we have seen party members suffer considerably. The new approach must now be in support of self-reliance and the creation of opportunities within the community itself, being facilitated, of course, by the new policies of our government.

With a measure of pride, I noted our political leader's comments earlier this week during GIS press conference, shared jointly with Sir Neville Nicholls, president of the Caribbean Development Bank (CDB). The prime minister spoke about the 1999-2001 CBD Country Strategy for Saint Lucia and said, "Our expectations are reflected in the fact that an indicative amount of approximately US$67.1 million has been set aside for project financing in Saint Lucia over the strategy period."

The prime minister was very clear on government's social development thrust being undertaken during that strategy period. He stated and I quote: "The principal economic objectives of the agreed strategy for Saint Lucia are the following: export diversification, human resource development, poverty reduction, environmental protection, and infrastructure development. The projects to be financed under the strategy are particularly important to our overall thrust to restructure the economy and position Saint Lucia on a path of sustainable growth in what is being dubbed the 'post-preferences era.'"

I am particularly pleased to note that government was very serious about social development as reflected in the provisions for human resource development and poverty reduction, for which an allocation of US$6 million will go towards the Basic Education Reform Program in order to create further expansion of our primary and senior-primary school system.

In this regard, we must seek to empower and enlighten our constituents so that together we may all become more productive, self-reliant, and as a result, depending less on the government for our livelihood. This basic political principle helps to send a positive message to all the people in this constituency and indeed, every Saint Lucian who truly loves this beloved country of ours. Therefore, it must be stated very forcefully, that the business of leadership must be taken seriously at both the community and national levels. This means that we must change the old ways of conducting our affairs.

Vieux Fortians, you have a most blessed economic community with tremendous potential, and recognizing this, you should take the opportunity to assist in the further development of your community. The infrastructure is already there to provide this economic boost. You have world-class international airport and sea port facilities. The honourable prime minister has taken the initiative to create further economic opportunities by negotiating for the development of a 250-room hotel for your community.

As you know, tourism is the backbone of our economy and the political leader has said and I quote: "The tourism industry must fill the void, create jobs, and earn foreign exchange needed by the economy." Further, in the 1998-1999 budget statement, the prime minister said, "It is government's philosophical position that tourism must benefit as many people as possible so that it may remain relevant, sustainable, and profitable for all stakeholders." Therefore, it is my call to your constituency group to prepare the mindset of your constituents to play a more meaningful role in this development thrust. There are tremendous opportunities available to the people of the community who are willing to work hard and to earn a living from the tourism industry. Our political leader will no doubt be assisting this constituency in realizing this potential.

Tourism must be our only hope for economic survival as it generates the hard currency needed to develop the economy. But without proper training and investment in human resource development, the tourism sector may fall short in achieving its fullest potential in earning that hard currency.

As a people, we must change our thinking to coincide with this new governance and to take advantage of the many opportunities becoming available in the community, so that we can develop our community on the Comfort 2000 concept, which is further enhanced by the projects being undertaken under the Poverty Reduction Fund (PRF), the Basic Needs Trust Fund, and other government initiatives. The whole idea is to encourage our communities to help themselves and to "build from the ground up."

This is the challenge that all constituency groups face throughout this country. As constituents you must get up, become useful and productive, or suffer the consequences of not exercising our personal initiative and developing niche markets for home-grown products and services.

When you look around, you will realize the neglect that has taken place throughout the various communities, perhaps because of a serious lack of political vision. We lack proper sporting facilities for our children. We need proper schools to educate our children so that they can contribute to the next generation of Saint Lucians who will lead this community. We also need proper roads, drains, and housing within the community in order to improve the quality of life of our people. In the final analysis, we all depend on each other to survive in this harsh economic climate. This is the reality!

Political Speech, Vieux Fort

Our energies must never be spent back-biting one another, but instead, elevating one another. We must be prepared to recondition our minds and to redirect ourselves to the cause of humanity. This constituency group must provide the framework and the leadership to guide and direct creative and innovative energies. We can and must make a difference by changing our negative mentality and ways. I ask you to support and defend your party, your government, your parliamentary representative, and your community. So I would further ask that you embrace the opportunity that this constituency is privileged to have: the honourable prime minister as your parliamentary representative.

In closing, I would encourage members of this constituency group to always engage in serious dialogue and to frequently consult your parliamentary representative on matters of critical importance to the community as a whole. You must also help one another to achieve your goals, dreams, and aspirations, in "Keeping Alive Grassroots Community Spirit."

chapter twenty-six

ADVICE FOR SAINT LUCIA

The following is a speech that I gave in Saint Lucia outlining some of my thoughts and observations for the way forward for Saint Lucia.

I wish to state categorically that based on my personal knowledge, experience, and empirical evidence, the old and wise saying "a prophet is never honoured in his own country" definitely applies to my native land, Saint Lucia.

Indeed, it is a country that pays very scant regard to our deserving citizens who have accomplished their goals by dint of hard work and perseverance. It is also true to say that Saint Lucians, especially those from rural communities like myself, are always blatantly discouraged by our own people, no matter how noble and excellent the cause.

This is an unfortunate fact that continues to impact negatively on the lives of many Saint Lucians and progressively stultify and stagnate their personal growth and development as they journey through the hazardous corridors of life and experiencing as it were, those inevitable vicissitudes and worldly trials and errors.

As a native Saint Lucian, who was born in the rural community of Anse La Raye, my whole life is a living testimony of personal endurance typical of the ordinary Saint Lucian folk. Generally speaking, it has been a life of continuous struggle in my humble attempts to survive and duly pursue a successful and professional career path.

In fact, the mere transition from suburban to glittering urban city life between the late 1950s to the early 1960s had its fair share of reckoning—as my personal experience had proven. In those colonial days, it was a difficult and bold step for a rural kid to venture into Castries, the capital city, in pursuit of career opportunities and to make for a better life.

Ebb and Flow

Therefore, by all stretch of one's imagination it was a difficult task to qualify and gain entry into the Royal Saint Lucia Police Force, given the required discipline and other stringent criteria. In fact, the discipline then imposed on young police officers like myself certainly prepared me for my subsequent professional development in the life insurance industry. But my professional life has not been easy and smooth sailing. But with regimented discipline and perseverance I endured.

It was former Saint Lucian Prime Minister Sir John Compton, who once publicly commented at a party political meeting that "The enemy is within." That political comment had fully awakened me to the reality of the Saint Lucian experience, in that I came to realize that as compatriots we were our greatest enemy.

As I journeyed through my personal and professional life, it became more and more obvious to me that as a Saint Lucian people we destroy rather than build one another. Indeed, we have nurtured a destructive culture where there is absolutely no compassion nor recognition of our very own people. We have a passion for bringing down and destroying one another, and we do not encourage one another to be successful.

In fact, we are very suspicious of the successes and strides being made by our compatriots by repeatedly casting aspersions and openly denigrating one another. Regrettably, what we have in Saint Lucia is an endemic culture of destruction and oppression. We seek to destroy our very own families, children, daughters, sons, brothers, sisters, cousins, nephews, nieces, wives and husbands, and even our common-law partners.

As a businessman, I have had several bad experiences of ingratitude displayed by the very native people of this country who come repeatedly on bended knees begging for job opportunities. As soon as they are employed, their cultural social habits seem to seek to destroy the very business that provides a daily bread for them, by reporting to work very late and being unproductive on the job.

They also plunder and pilfer with impunity. Apart from stealing in broad daylight, they also maliciously destroy the good reputation of their employers in cunning ways that are beyond the imagination; thereby making employer and employee relations adversarial and not conducive to proper human resource development initiatives. The workplace has been transformed into a breeding ground of perpetual hostility and a tug-of-war between employer and employee. In fact, this situation is now going through a degenerative process.

On the other hand, the government is not helping to appease the situation because it is putting undue pressure on local entrepreneurs and local business

Advice for Saint Lucia

enterprises by creating unnecessary foreign competition. In many cases, foreign investors do have a distinct competitive advantage over local investors in terms of tax-free holidays and other concessions being accorded to foreign investors. Saint Lucian local industries can attest to the fact that the playing field is not level. Local entrepreneurs do suffer tremendous losses compared to their foreign counterparts, whose profit margins far exceed those of local businesses.

This economic imbalance in the marketplace must be addressed with some urgency by the relevant authorities before it is too late. Government must play its vital role of effectively administering, regulating, and monitoring the local economy and thereby removing all the unnecessary bottlenecks that are impeding the economic progress of many Saint Lucian entrepreneurs.

However, it is my humble view that while many Saint Lucians continue to fight among themselves, there seems to be more solidarity and togetherness within the expatriate group. In fact, the majority of Saint Lucians do benefit a lot more from foreigners than their own compatriots who are bent on destroying each other through envy, jealousy, greed, and covetousness.

There seems to be a tendency among our people to express venom rather than human compassion and love for one another. But I am happy to report that my best friends in this country are the expatriates who have always encouraged me in my business and professional endeavours.

Therefore, as a Saint Lucian people, we must unite now and put aside our narrow-mindedness, pettiness, and destructive attitude. As a nation, we become poorer and poorer by perpetuating that woefully destructive and divisive culture. That cultural behaviour should be a thing of the past.

In the new millennium, we must rise confidently to the challenge of eliminating those evil deeds of the past that are no longer a part of the new Saint Lucian communal and entrepreneurial spirit and start to recognize excellence and hard work without prejudicial and insularity trappings that were once characteristic of small island states like Saint Lucia.

I now sound the clarion call to wake up and usher in that new Saint Lucian spirit based on true patriotism and camaraderie.

chapter twenty-seven

HOSPITALITY INDUSTRY SPEECH

I was president of the Saint Lucia Hotel and Tourism Association when I gave the following address. The occasion was the Second Biennial Hospitality Industry Conference.

Mr. Noel Cadasse, President of the Saint Lucia Hotel and Tourism Association at the Second Biennial Hospitality Industry Conference and Annual General Meeting held on Friday, November 1, 1996 at Sandals Saint Lucia

Let me take this opportunity to welcome you to the open session of our Second Biennial Hospitality Industry Conference. Special welcome to our invited guests who have made the effort to share their morning with us—we appreciate your coming. On behalf of the members and myself, I say special welcome to our Caribbean hotelier and colleague, Peter Rousseau, for agreeing to be our guest today to deliver the feature address this morning. Peter is a very prominent and active campaigner for the hotel industry in the region, and we are fortunate that he could find the time to share some of his enormous experience with us this morning. Peter, we wish you a very pleasant stay.

I also extend my own welcome to the honourable minister of tourism—who I must admit has always been keen to add his support to the activities and programs of the association. To our members, I extend special greetings and we are looking forward to engaging your collective wisdom to guide the decisions of the association at the Annual General Meeting that follows this opening session.

Our association is nothing more than a voluntary coming together of a group of people to solve common problems, meet common goals. In pursuance of these general objectives, we endeavour to remain steadfastly focused on satisfying the needs of our membership. We accept that an effective association is one which recognizes and focuses on the common self-interests of its members, and we shall continue to work in that direction, to increase membership satisfaction and membership benefits.

But in this dynamic world of ever-changing conditions, the common needs of the membership do not remain constant. Changes in the marketplace caused by technological impact and other evolving conditions require the association to respond to these changes and to adapt as well as to adopt programs and create priorities so that the association can retain its effectiveness. It therefore requires the association to play a leadership role, by becoming a more knowledge-based organization, supported by a professionally trained and highly motivated executive and staff engaged in providing the enabling conditions for continuous and integrated consideration of:

* Membership needs;
* The strategic position of the association; and
* The dynamics and realities of the external marketplace.

During my tenure as president and chairman of the board of directors, over the last twenty-four months or so, we have attempted to move in that direction. The difficulty has been to engage the various sectors of the association in constant dialogue. There seems to be an attitude of leaving it to the executive to make the right judgment and decisions on their behalf.

This coming board of directors will have to find a new formula to engage the various sectors in more constant dialogue, in order to create that integrated consideration that is crucial to maintaining our effectiveness as an association.

The theme of this conference, "Positioning the Industry for the Twenty-first Century," demands that we set the necessary foundations, create the suitable conditions that will put the industry on the right path to face the challenges that lay ahead, and to turn these new challenges into new opportunities. We hope we have begun this process in the formulation of a draft strategic plan to guide the direction of the association. The main goals, objectives, and strategies will be presented to the general membership later today at the closed session for their approval.

Let me continue by giving a brief summary of the performance of the industry. For the past four years, tourism arrivals have gone up significantly each year. In 1994-1995 season, we saw a record percentage increase of 12.5 percent, with the US market growing by 35 percent. This year we anticipate

Hospitality Industry Speech

less dramatic increases, but the figures for the first eight months of this year indicate a 5 percent improvement on the number of stay-over arrivals over the corresponding period last year. However, the majority of our member hotels experienced a very soft summer, causing average occupancy figures to decline from 64.5 percent to 62.5 percent. The non all-inclusive and the small hotel sector went along with the tide, recording declines in average occupancy. The all-inclusive hotel sector, however, went against this trend in continuing to record high occupancies and increased from 76 percent to 78 percent.

The decline in hotel occupancy can be attributed to the successive decline in arrivals in the months of June, July, and August from our biggest tourism market—the United States of America—resulting in a net decline of 4.2 percent up to August 1996. The decline in this market has been attributed to the Summer Olympic Games, which was staged in Atlanta this year, and to the election year in the US, which always has a negative impact on consumers' holiday travel. The UK market, on the other hand, our second-most-important market, while it recorded net gains of 1.7 percent for the first eight months of 1996, successive declines from that market in the months of July and August of 8.9 percent and 3.8 percent respectively also contributed to this very soft summer.

Arrivals from the Canadian market remain consistent by recording further declines in the period under consideration, although recent development in that market to which I will refer later is giving us new hope and optimism for that market. While there were significant percentage increases from the German and French markets in Europe, because these markets are relatively small for us, the percentage increase translates into small numbers.

The biggest increase for the first eight months of this year has come from the Caribbean market, where the month of August recorded over 10,000 arrivals, more than 40 percent of that number coming from Martinique.

However, our research indicates that total room revenue accruing to the hotel sector declined for the period under consideration. This was caused by the fall in average occupancies, the closure of Jalousie Plantation Resort, and the renovations being carried out at some major hotels together with the fact that average room rates have declined approximately 12 percent over last summer's rates.

We believe, however, that this is only a temporary situation and the industry is looking forward to a good winter season. Saint Lucia maintains a very good reputation with our overseas wholesale tour operators. Our optimism is further enhanced by the new marketing initiatives being taken by the Saint

Ebb and Flow

Lucia Tourist Board and us in which we are confident that we are heading for a good tourism season.

At our last general meeting in December, I drew the attention of the membership to our dependence on the size of our airlift capacity and the performance of the hotel sector and urged that greater efforts be made to attract additional air capacity. I am pleased to report that developments in that area add to our optimism for the future of the industry. Last Friday, we witnessed the inaugural flight of Air Liberte bringing in over 300 visitors on a direct flight from Paris.

This flight is the end result of discussions that began in London in November last year while we were at World Travel Market and concluded in April this year when the then chairman of the airline came to Saint Lucia to meet with ourselves and the tourist board to finalize details. This flight will provide direct service every Friday from Paris using an airbus with a capacity of 316 seats. This direct service out of Paris provides our tourism industry with the opportunity to intensify our marketing with our tour operators in France to develop the French market in the way we always thought we could.

This month we will also have two new weekly charter flights out of Canada. One of the flights is originating out of Montreal, which gives us a great opportunity to exploit the French Canadian market. The other flight is coming out of Toronto, our more traditional tourism-generating region in Canada. These two new flights out of Canada will give us the opportunity to reverse the declining numbers we have been experiencing out of this market.

Air Jamaica's proposals to fly out of New York and Atlanta, and the possibility of discussing other routes with the airline, gives us great hope for the future. We are particularly anxious to work with Air Jamaica on the Atlanta route, to develop the marketing of the southeast United States. We wish to express our thanks to the government of Saint Lucia for committing US$500,000 to the promotional and marketing efforts in support of the flights.

From the United Kingdom, successful discussions have been held with Air Tours, the second largest tour operators in the UK, and we are expecting a new charter flight starting next summer out of Gatwick. We are now in the process of making some proposals to BWIA, which has recently reinstated its flights into Saint Lucia out of Miami and New York.

With the new business plan proposed by BWIA for putting flights where they are needed for the tourist market, we are now formulating proposals to submit to the airline to provide charter service out of specific markets we would like to see develop.

Hospitality Industry Speech

These are some of the positives we can see developing in the airline sector, but we remain concerned with the over-dependence on American Airlines, which I must admit has been a great partner and supporter of our tourism industry. However, the near-monopoly situation and its connection with the major American wholesale tour operators that supply Saint Lucia, the airline continues to have a tremendous influence over the cost of a holiday to Saint Lucia. The airline has recently announced that bulk fares to the Caribbean are going up by some 20 percent, which is not something that we are looking forward to. But we are hoping that with the additional competition we intend to attract on the US market routes, we will support greater price stability.

Ladies and gentlemen, this year cannot be described as a normal year. It was a year in which we saw a change in the government of Saint Lucia with the appointment of a new prime minister. It was also one in which we saw increased unrest in the banana industry, with a number of no-cut strikes by the banana farmers causing major setbacks to the industry and the economy. The Copra-Manufacturing Company going into receivership and the closure of the Jalousie Plantation Resort added to our economic woes.

The changes that are affecting the performance of business in Saint Lucia are a reflection of our tardy response to changes in the marketing conditions. This is the problem with which the banana industry is faced. Over the years the industry has failed to position itself to these market changes, and the unrest in the industry is merely a symptom of this negligence.

The challenge for the long-term survival of the export market for our bananas in Europe has little to do with the composition of the board of directors of the Banana Association and even less to do with the date of the Banana Farmers Conference. The long-term survival of the banana export market lies with the ability of the industry to produce a good quality banana at a price that is competitive on the international market. And that is where our energies and resources should be directed—so that when the concessionary arrangements that allow us to export our fruit to the British market come to an end, we will be in a position to hold our own on the international market.

The impending loss of our banana export market is a two-edged sword. On the positive side, it can bring benefits to the association as it increases the clout of the tourism sector because of the increasing reliance on tourism for the country's economic well-being. On the negative side, the loss of jobs in the banana Industry can lead to social unrest, which can impact negatively on tourist arrivals. It is therefore in the interest of the Saint Lucia Hotel and Tourism

Association to encourage greater inter-sector linkages, particularly in the agricultural sector.

While we have taken the initiative with the Adopt-A-Farmer Program, which made a significant contribution to increasing direct purchases from a number of local farmers involved in the program, the time has come for a coordinated national plan to stimulate agricultural development away from bananas. We do not have a choice in this matter. The reality of the external marketing forces will force many banana farmers out of production, and those displaced farmers will have to find some alternative means of making a living. The millions of dollars the government is committing every week to subsidize banana farmers, including those farmers that will be forced out of the industry, could be better spent in assisting those farmers in making the transition.

The Saint Lucia Marketing Board, which was formed to encourage local agricultural production, imports 85 percent of its stock, while the hotel industry is frequently faced with shortages of basic food items such as cucumbers, lettuce, and other vegetables. We are at an important crossroad in the evolution of the tourism industry, and the time is now for us to approach the development of the sector in a holistic manner. And agriculture must play a key role in the inter-sectoral linkage. We do not know how many times we need to make this point, but so far our pleas seemed to have been largely ignored—there have been no significant measures taken to move in that direction—apart from the Adopt-A-Farmer program introduced by the association.

The theme of this conference is "Positioning the Industry for the Twenty-first Century." This is a timely theme but one which the banana industry has ignored, and the result is instability in the industry, which poses a threat to tourism sector and the economy. We in the tourism industry cannot afford to repeat the mistakes of the banana industry. The window of opportunity is now open for the private and public sectors to form a strategic alliance to position the industry to face the new challenges ahead.

Let me now attempt to identify some of the areas that require the attention of the public sector in that regard. I have already identified the need to strengthen the linkage between agriculture and tourism. The role of the public sector is to provide a regime of incentives to both farmers and hoteliers and to encourage the use of local agricultural products. This incentive package should include soft loans to be made available to finance banana farmers to make the transition from bananas to vegetable and fruit production.

Hospitality Industry Speech

Another area that needs urgent review is the present regime of the incentive legislation. While the association supported the new Tourism Incentive Act, which was passed into law in March this year to replace Hotel Ordinance of 1959, the new act, while it provides for the main suppliers of the tourism product an opportunity to access some fiscal incentives—which was an improvement on the old legislation, which recognized only hotels for that purpose—the new legislation, like the old one, concentrates on incentives as a means of attracting new investments.

However a recent study commissioned by CTO on Caribbean tourism sector taxation has come to the conclusion that no "discernable link can be detected between the level of incentives offered and the increase in hotel investment." The study went on to state that there are even more important factors to be considered, including the overall commitment to tourism and marketing and the supporting infrastructural network.

The best way to attract new investments is by creating the environment that will make the tourism sector profitable. A 1995 report on the financial performance of the Caribbean hotels revealed that the sector was unprofitable, operating at a net loss of over US$2,000 per room. The conclusion of that report should force us to engage in meaningful dialogue as to how the present taxation system affects the profitability of the industry. And also, for hoteliers to find ways to reduce costs without compromising quality service.

We need also to critically examine the administration of the tourism industry in order to be more cost effective and increase accountability. The present structure of the Saint Lucia Tourist Board and the Ministry of Tourism needs some review. We would like to suggest that the Ministry of Tourism assume the non-marketing functions now being performed by the Saint Lucia Tourist Board and to dedicate the Saint Lucia Tourist Board to marketing and promoting Saint Lucia as a tourist destination. The organization should be renamed the Tourism Marketing Corporation, or some similar name to better reflect its new role. The board of this marketing organization should be a high-powered one, where the members are selected from experienced hoteliers and businesspersons on the island, who would bring to the table the benefits of their collective experiences.

In the case of the Ministry of Tourism, we believe that it should be a stand-alone ministry assuming the functions of product development and the public education programs for the industry, which are performed by the Tourist Board, and in the interest of cost-effectiveness and efficiency to determine what aspects of these functions could be contracted out. In addition, the ministry assumes responsibility for the following:

* To provide the facility for consultation to help carve the vision for the industry and to create mechanisms and allocate the resources to achieve that vision;
* To play a major role in investment promotion for the sector and to develop investment strategies to attract new hotels; and
* To be the regulatory body for the industry with responsibility for maintaining standards.

At this point in time, the responsibility of performing these functions, which is vital to the development of the industry, is not readily determined. We cannot position the industry to enter the next century under an administrative structure that may have been relevant twenty years ago, but may not necessarily meet the needs of a modern industry.

This brings me to another critical area in which urgent action has to be taken—and this has to do with the financial resources required for the promotion and marketing of Saint Lucia as a tourism destination. Under the existing agreement, the government provides the marketing funds available to the tourist board. But in spite of the act, the industry has become the number-one export industry, contributing over $250 million US dollars annually to our foreign exchange earnings. The marketing dollars provided to the tourist board by the government accounts for less than one percent of the industry's contribution to foreign exchange earnings.

Last year, we met with the Ministry of Tourism to discuss new ways of providing additional funds for the marketing and promotion of Saint Lucia, and in fact, the minister appointed a committee under the chairmanship of the late Peter Bergasse to report on a way of funding the industry. One of the last functions performed by Peter Bergasse on behalf of the industry, before he passed away in July last year, was to present findings of this report to the minister in which far-reaching recommendations were made, including the creation of a tourism-development fund to assist in marketing the industry. This entity would be funded from the private sector, and government would provide generous tax allowances to the subscribers of these funds. We are hoping that this year we can have further dialogue on this matter with the government.

Other areas we need to deal with are related to the small hotel sector, where we must develop special institutional and legislative mechanisms to create a

Hospitality Industry Speech

profitable environment for that sector. The creation of the Inns of Saint Lucia program and, more recently, the classification of the small hotels into groups depending on the type of assistance required is providing great help to the small hotels sector. We need to do more and the hotel association is looking at the possibility of creating a bulk-purchasing program to help reduce costs of operations for the small hotels.

On the issue of crime, we persuaded the government to create an advisory committee, but to date the committee has not been able to achieve very much. That is not because the committee is inactive but because the recommendations require government support and have implications for the government's budget. But this continues to be a critical area of concern for us, and we are still hoping that in the government's new budgetary proposals, they will take into account the measures proposed by the advisory committee.

When I became president of the association, I wanted to make staff training and education the cornerstone of my tenure. I had the dream of making every taxi driver an ambassador for the country, well trained and committed to providing professional service. I wanted to see the immigration officers welcome visitors with a genuine smile, while they were assisting in a professional and efficient manner in the processing of their immigration papers. I had the dream that the customs officers, while performing their tasks in an uncompromising and professional way, would see the tourists as customers to be given the best service. I wanted to see every tour guide sufficiently knowledgeable about the product so as to provide our visitors with an unforgettable experience. I had a dream where every hotel worker would approach their job with such friendliness and efficiency that the quality of service at our hotels would be the envy of the world.

I may not achieve all my dreams in that area, but I am happy that all the hotels in Saint Lucia have placed tremendous effort and resources to staff training and development. The commitment to increasing the quality of service through improving the skills of the workers in the industry is a trend that will continue to grow. I am happy to see the increasing number of Saint Lucians who now hold managerial positions at member hotels. This augurs well for the future of our industry.

Ladies and gentlemen, the structure of the tourism industry is such that there is need for continuous cooperation and dialogue between the industry and the public sector. We are convinced that we must work together to achieve the best for the industry. In that regard, we have established, especially in the last few years, a good working relationship with the Ministry of Tourism as well as the Saint Lucia Tourist Board. Never in the history of our tourism development have we had such an excellent relationship, and for this I want to place on record my association's appreciation and gratitude to the minister of tourism for the exciting and productive relationship that we have enjoyed with his ministry. His continuous support and quick responses to our requests have certainly made my task as president less difficult.

In closing, ladies and gentlemen, it would be remiss of me if I did not say special thanks to all our members for their support during the last two years.

When the minister of tourism addressed us last year he asked the questions: "Can we afford to be without a viable tourism industry? With the problems of the banana industry and the decline of the manufacturing business in Saint Lucia, can we survive without tourism? This is the question I put to hotel workers, taxi drivers, restaurant owners, shop owners, farmers, fishermen, day boat charter operators, dock workers, airline workers, and others. I ask, can Saint Lucia do without the tourism industry?"

I ask the question now: can Saint Lucia afford to be without this tourism industry?

The chairman of the Saint Lucia Tourist Board and the director of tourism have given us tremendous cooperation and support, providing the opportunity for frequent consultation on the various issues that came up over the last two years. I am particularly grateful to Ms. Agnes Francis for the excellent work she is doing at the tourist board and by extension, to her staff especially the work now being done in the small hotel sector and the Statistical Department of the board.

Let me take the opportunity to thank Executive Vice President Mr. Hilary Modeste for his unflinching support and the professional approach he brought to bear on the work of the association and to extend my thanks also the rest of his team, Eileen, Phyllis, Alice, Deline, and Nika, a hardworking team of individuals who have made my task as president less stressful.

Ladies and gentlemen, I want to officially advise the membership that I do not intend to seek re-election as president. The last two years have been enjoyable ones. It was hard work, but I dedicated myself to doing what I had to do, and whenever I was called upon to act on behalf of the association, I was always there. But the time has come for me to pass on the baton to someone else to continue to build on what we have achieved. It was an honour to serve as president, and I will continue to be a member of the board as Immediate Past

Hospitality Industry Speech

President, where I will be able to share my experiences with the new board. I will continue to be frank, as in the words of the minister, "Be not afraid to speak out, for this is your country, your industry."

When I accepted the honour of serving you, I knew the challenges ahead. The minister of tourism in his address to this body reminded me again that I should accept the office to serve with honour and not for honour. Ladies and gentlemen, you are my judge.

As we approach a new year, let me on behalf of my family wish you God's richest blessings for a very pleasant holiday season and to wish you a prosperous tourism season.

chapter twenty-eight

AGRITOUR SPEECH

My expertise in the tourism industry means that I developed a broad-based vision and development plan for the tourism sector. Here is another speech that outlines my ideas.

Address by Noel N.S. Cadasse, President of the Saint Lucia Hotel and Tourism Association (SLHTA) at AgriTour '95 at the Wyndham Morgan Bay Resort on February 8, 1995

It is a real pleasure for me to be here today to join hands with the farmers and administrators in the agricultural sector and the other organizations, such as CARDI, the French Technical Mission, and others in this consultation named AgriTour '95, in the continuing efforts at strengthening the linkages between the hospitality industry and the agricultural sector.

Let me, on behalf of the Saint Lucia Hotel and Tourism Association commend the Saint Lucia Marketing Board for taking the initiative in organizing this consultative forum. I hope that this gathering here today will result in the implementation of new and positive steps to escalate the process towards the goal of achieving and agricultural industry in which the farmers are sensitized and equipped with the necessary support systems and mechanisms to begin to satisfy the growing demand for local fruits, vegetables, and herbs in our expanding hospitality sector.

The Hotel and Tourism Association has been trying, through its "Adopt-A-Farmer" program, in forging the link with the local farmers, to create the opportunity for them to produce the quality and quantity demanded by the industry. We have had some modest success in this new and bold venture. The farmers involved in the Adopt-A-Farmer project have had the opportunity to establish a good working relationship with the chefs and the food and beverage managers of the hotels to develop the quality produce required by the hotels and also to generally sensitize and educate the farmers to the needs of the industry. I know in some cases, the food and beverage people of the hotels have visited the farms of their adopted farmer to assist the farmer in quality control and other matters.

We have been able to establish a good relationship with the French Mission, who have been working closely with many of the farmers who are involved in the scheme. I wish to go on record to convey my sincere gratitude to the French Mission, through the French Ambassador, Madame Silvie Alvarez, for the assistance being given to the Saint Lucia garners in diversifying their production and assisting them in new production techniques, such as greenhouse production.

As I have said earlier, the Adopt-A-Farmer project has had some success. In fact, at the recent National Hospitality Awards, we were able to recognize the most successful farmers in the project. But we realize that this project has its limitations, and it is necessary for us now to establish a national thrust to escalate the process towards an agricultural sector completely diversified to meet the needs of the industry.

AgriTour '95 should be initiating that thrust. This consultation should be about identifying the practical steps needed for strengthening the ties between the agricultural sector and the hospitality industry. It should be about providing useful information to the farmers of Saint Lucia to demonstrate the need for crop diversification. This AgriTour '95 should be defining solutions—not only identifying the problems and difficulties, but look for practical solutions to solve the issue of crop diversification. This forum here today should be about defining the role of the Saint Lucia Marketing Board and to examine how the board could act as the main catalyst as a marketing organization to accelerate the process of diversification.

Our deliberations here today must also seriously address the role of the education system in cementing the linkages between agriculture and tourism. Young people being trained for the job market must be trained in the areas where our economic fortunes lie. For a number of years now, statistics have been revealing that tourism is the fastest growing sector of the economy, presenting numerous opportunities for the agricultural sector. In spite of this, there has not been any inclination on the part of education authorities to reform the school curriculum to enable young people to grasp the available opportunities. This consultation must endeavour to get education authorities to also act.

AgriTour Speech

Measured in terms of foreign exchange earnings, tourism is the largest industry in the Caribbean. Last year approximately fourteen million stay-over visitors came to the Caribbean, and there were another 9 million who came as day excursionists and from cruise ships with an estimated expenditure of over 12 billion US dollars.

Saint Lucia continues to hold its own in the Caribbean tourism market. In 1994, stay-over arrivals increased by 12.5 percent over the previous year to 218,000. In other words, during the last twelve months, an additional number of people amounting to almost twice the population of Saint Lucia were here to be fed with food and drink. And this figure is expected to grow, as more rooms are added to our existing inventory. And with a more aggressive advertising and promotion campaign, we expect stay-over arrivals to almost double by the beginning of the new century.

So there we are, faced with this massive and growing market—are we ready to take advantage of the market possibilities afforded to the agricultural sector? How ready are the farmers? Are they fully sensitized and educated to the growing needs of the hospitality industry—the need to diversify into the non-traditional crops to produce the quantities, quality, and varieties demanded by a sophisticated tourism industry? Is the marketing board ready and equipped as a marketing agency to instil confidence in the farmers that their production will be sold at a good price? Is the Ministry of Agriculture ready to provide the support mechanisms to provide the sort of extension service to the farmers, to educate and provide the technical know-how to assist the farmers to overcome their production difficulties? Are we ready to take advantage of the assistance being offered by CARDI, the French Mission, for technical cooperation as well as the assistance offered by the Chinese authorities to maximize and absorb that assistance in our quest for crop diversification? These are some of the questions that must be answered today to come up with some practical solutions.

The Saint Lucia Hotel and Tourism Association has been ready to give its full support in creating a diversified agricultural sector to meet the demands of the hospitality industry. We have demonstrated this through our Adopt-A-Farmer Program and the recent donation of nearly $65,000 worth of seeds from this hotel to assist the farmers in their rehabilitation efforts following the passage of Storm Debbie last September.

I hope that today will be a major landmark in establishing the conditions of readiness that are necessary to forge that necessary link between the hospitality industry and agriculture. We cannot afford to fail—and as we look ahead, with an uncertain future facing the banana industry, it becomes even more urgent to come up with a full-time commitment to the agricultural diversification process.

I know we have the will: today we must strengthen the determination.

American Airlines (April 15, 1999)

There is so much happening in the air transportation sector. It is now common knowledge that the American Airlines direct service out of Miami will cease to operate as of April 15th. I cannot help but think that perhaps a more favourable outcome might have been achieved had the government in a more thorough dialogue at the highest level, with the principles of American Airlines, on their request for direct support, vis-à-vis the destination's preferred approach of an expanded cooperative marketing program.

Having said this, however, the association is hopeful that we can work very closely with the tourist board in their efforts at securing additional charter services and in their marketing program, to ensure that any adverse impacts of the withdrawal of the American Airlines service are minimized.

The response of Air Jamaica and BWIA are encouraging, and we are all hopeful that the recent investments by these two regional carriers will result in a net increase in airline seats for Saint Lucia and the region as a whole, more competitively priced air fares, and more stable and reliable air transportation in the medium to long term.

Hotel Operating Costs

The hotel sector is now engaged in various tourism programs such as cost reduction, improved maintenance scheduling and increased efficiency in the use of water energy, which will impact positively on the bottom line. At the national level, there are some changes that are taking place in which the association has been participating, which will impact on hotel operating costs. I refer in particular to reforms in the telecommunications and water sectors.

The association took part in the national stakeholder consultation on the reform of the telecommunications sector. We intend to follow this up by inviting a representative of the regional consultants on this project to address interested sections of our membership on the implications of the reform for reduced telecommunications costs and expanded services. Interested members are asked to contact the secretariat.

Regarding the changes in the water sector, I have already alerted the government to the fact that the association is aware that the move towards according

AgriTour Speech

corporate status to WASA, now to be known as the Water and Sewerage Company (WASCO), is bound to lead to some increase in water rates. As members would be aware, under the existing regime of water tariffs, companies are already charged a much higher rate than domestic users.

I have argued that since we are already paying those higher rates, which are close to the true cost of producing and distributing water, the ordinary household must now be called upon to play its fair share of that cost. The brunt of the burden should not be made to fall on the commercial sector; otherwise an undesirable situation will arise where the private sector will be directly subsidizing the consumption of water by the household sector. We trust that WASCO and the government will take this consideration fully into account when devising the new tariff regime.

Of immediate concern to many hoteliers, particularly in the north, is the temporary shortage of water resulting form the need to ration the limited supply. We are already in discussion with WASA/WASCO concerning measures that could be taken to alleviate this situation in the short term and resolve it within the next year.

Another form of intervention, which holds out many opportunities for reduction in operating costs, is the establishment of strategic alliances involving our members. We are currently awaiting further information on a strategic alliance which is being negotiated by the CHA at a regional level with Tropical Shipping in Miami. Under this arrangement, discounts for bulk importation will be available, together with a facility for short-term credit. Members will be informed in due course of the details of this initiative. We also hope to cultivate a relationship with American Express that would be conducive to the development of a strategic alliance with that company.

At the local level, the association will be looking for opportunities to foster greater collaboration among members in their purchasing operations. We are calling on the various segments of our membership, including our allied members, to suggest possibilities for joint purchasing which the association could assist in coordinating or facilitating. One example that has been suggested is cleaning products. We are also extending an invitation to the Chamber of Commerce to link up with the SLHTA in this initiative.

Water-Based Tourism

I would just like to make a few pointed statements about developments in this sector, which continue to show a great deal of potential. We are pleased to announce that the government has agreed to allocate a reasonable sum of money towards meeting the cost of establishing a hyperbaric or decompression chamber for the benefit of divers and fishermen. I am aware that the Dive Association has also pledged a financial commitment to that facility. I want to take this opportunity to signal the commitment of the SLHTA to this project, and to throw out the challenge to the hotel sector to make an initial financial contribution as well to the project.

Notice that I have not made an undertaking on behalf of the sector to pay. The association has learned from recent experience the risk in making such commitments, however laudable the cause might be. I have merely appealed to the good judgment and self-interest of hoteliers with dive operations to support this worthwhile initiative. I must also applaud the efforts of the tourist board in providing more visibility in the marketplace of Saint Lucia's dive product.

Let me also commend the Ministry of Tourism for establishing and chairing a working committee in the yachting sector. The association intends to become more active in representing the interests of its members in the yachting sector on this committee.

Before moving to the next sector, I want to acknowledge the difficulties that some day boat charter operators have been experiencing with the distribution of business in this area. This is not a straightforward matter to deal with, but I want to let our day boat charter members know that the association will not pretend that a problem does not exist. We are committed to doing all that is within our influence to help with a solution to your grievances. We hope that the open forum this afternoon will provide you with an opportunity to elaborate on the difficulties that you face and help us to fashion a clearer perspective on the courses of corrective action open to all the players concerned.

Community-Based Tourism

Activity in the community-based tourism sector is on the rise. This is an area in which the association has not had an active presence, and we would like to change that. We are keen to support the initiatives of the community-based Nature Heritage Tourism Program and to present them. At the same time, I want to reiterate my call for more of our members with a community presence and who have business relations with community presence and who have business relations with community groups, to revive the Adopt-A-School and Adopt-A-Farmer programs.

AgriTour Speech

I want to take this opportunity to express the support of the association for the projects being developed for Anse La Raye, namely the botanical garden and the fish fry project. But while we forge ahead with new ventures aimed at including more and community-based activities. I refer in particular to activities in the Marigot area and in Gros-Islet.

I would like to offer the support the association in working with the Ministry of Tourism in reviewing the tourism-related activities in these two communities. This is firstly with a view to implementing some controls and measures to address the complaints that have been received form some of our guests, as well as residents and business places, regarding some of the negative and undesirable elements and impacts of the nightlife in these areas. Secondly we need to look together at ways of improving the quality of the product and the community experience offered to our visitors. It is good to be spontaneous, but the time has come for all the major tourism players to put some thought and action into the development of these communities urgently. Otherwise there is a real risk that they may self-destruct and the economic benefits to these communities will evaporate.

Sports Tourism

We at the association are looking forward to the formulation of a definitive government policy statement on sports tourism. We believe that there is a niche to be exploited here, and would be happy to work with the Ministry of Sports and the Ministry of Tourism in developing the opportunities in this area.

Entertainment

Another potential growth area is entertainment. One of the biggest complaints received by hotel general managers from their guests is that the entertainment on offer is poor in quality and limited in scope. Let me acknowledge the efforts of the Ministry of Tourism in mobilizing some of the players in the entertainment industry to come together to develop their industry. We believe that a broader and more coordinated effort is required, which ideally should involve the Ministry of Culture. In that regard, we derive some of the comfort from the emphasis placed by the minister of culture on the development of culture and the promotion of indigenous art forms. Witness the tremendous benefits that have been derived from the Jazz Master Classes, for instance.

It must also be remembered that our hotels serve an international clientele, and it is in the interest of tourism and the wider national interest of us to encourage the influx of new cultural experiences and forms of entertainment to enrich the visitor experience. In addition, an offering of quality entertainment is an integral component of the sort of quality tourism product which Saint Lucia needs to offer in order to remain competitive and to keep our room rates up at a reasonably high level. There is a slight concern that the proposed tax on entertainers might stymie the growth of entertainment in Saint Lucia. This possible impact must be studied carefully to ensure that the tax does not have any such unintended negative repercussions.

Synopsis of Accomplishments/Activities

I have attempted to provide members with a synopsis of the achievements of the association since the new board took up the reins of leadership in December last year. I have alluded to some of the activities in which the association will be engaged in the months ahead. Summaries are provided in your folios. We have also included a list of new members and prospective members. You will note that you will appreciate that the introduction of new activities and programs is a time-absorbing process, which we in many instances have little control over. I have also shared with you some of the new ideas that we are considering.

It should be evident by now that many of these proposals will either not come to fruition or will not have the impact that you our members desire without your feedback, active participation, and support. I therefore want to appeal to all of you to support your association, support the leadership, work with your sector directors and committee leaders, and cooperate with the secretariat, so that the association can provide you with the assistance and representation you need accordingly

Ladies and gentlemen, I know that I have spoken at length. I know, however, that you will forgive me since this is our first quarterly meeting for the year and the first opportunity that I have had to address the broader membership. Remember that your association can only be as strong as the input and support that you give to it. I trust that I have given a good account of the efforts of your association, and I look forward to your questions, comments, and contributions.

chapter twenty-nine

POLITICAL SPEECH

The following is a political speech I made in 1999.

"Brotherhood and Service in the Community": Welcome Remarks by Bro. Noel N.S. Cadasse, Chairman, Anse La Raye/Canaries Constituency Group, September 5, 1999

Brothers and sisters, it is indeed a very special pleasure and a privilege for me to welcome each and every one of you to our annual constituency conference and in particular to allow you the freedom of our village.

This annual conference provides an ideal forum and an opportunity for members of this Anse La Raye/Canaries Constituency Group to engage in serious thinking and reflection. We as a constituency earnestly strive to improve standards of our community and to provide the political leadership that is vital to the achievement of our goals, dreams, and aspirations. This constituency group is therefore able to play a pivotal role in providing the right kind of awareness and education that would assist in achieving these goals. Generally, we seek to empower and enlighten our constituents so that together we may all become more productive, self-reliant, and as a result, depending less on the government for our livelihood.

As outlined in the 1997 elections manifesto, the Saint Lucia Labour Party (SLP) in a clearly defined statement of principles, made its position very clear in respect to community development. That particular principle states quite clearly, and I quote. "Every community should be encouraged to assume greater responsibility for its own development. Every community should be empowered to protect the integrity of the environment and to ensure its sustainability."

This basic political principle helps to send a positive message to all the people in this constituency and, indeed, every Saint Lucian who truly loves this beloved country of ours. It must be brought home very forcefully that the business of leadership must be taken seriously at both the community and national levels. This means that we must change the old ways of conducting our affairs. Naturally, good governance is necessary if we are to remain alive in today's rapidly changing world.

The global economy is on the move, and absolutely no sympathy will be shown to struggling economies—economies that are clearly at a disadvantage in terms of modernizing their service industries and competing on a level playing field.

For example, Saint Lucia's tourism industry must be our only hope for economic survival, as it generates the hard currency needed to develop the local economy. Without proper training and continual investments in human resource development, the tourism industry may fall short in achieving its fullest potential in earning that hard currency. In essence, we must streamline our operations and modernize our economy if we are to be successful as a nation. Therefore as a people we must change our thinking and take the bull by the horns, if this becomes absolutely necessary.

In particular, as the traditional sources of foreign aid available to developing countries such as Saint Lucia are drying up, the lack of money will make it increasingly difficult for government to allocate funds for community development projects, be it in Anse La Raye, Canaries, or elsewhere. This is the hard-nosed reality we face as we approach the new century. Therefore, the citizens in our communities are required to be self-reliant, creative, innovative, and productive in whatever way possible. Community projects must be self-reliant and self-supporting in keeping with the concept of COMFORT 2000, which encourages our communities to help themselves and to "build from the ground up."

That is the challenge that all constituency groups face throughout this country. As constituents we must get up, become useful and productive, or suffer the consequences of not exercising our personal initiative and developing niche markets for home grown products and services. We must realize that handouts are no longer available or fashionable in the modern world. We must be able to think for ourselves and develop bankable proposals and also be able to present them convincingly and confidently to the bank so that money can be made available for worthy community projects. When we look around, we will observe that our communities have been neglected in a most shameful manner.

Political Speech

We lack proper facilities and amenities for our people in those communities. We need proper sporting facilities for our children. We need proper schools to educate our children so that they can contribute to the next generation of Saint Lucians who will lead this community. We also need proper roads, drains, and housing within the community in order to improve the quality of life of our people across the board. In the final analysis, we all depend on each other to survive in this harsh economic climate. So each one of us must pull our weight and put our shoulders to the wheel. This is the reality!

Similarly, we must become a more productive, progressive, and proactive country that means business. We can no longer afford to be in the laid-back mode expecting manna to fall from the sky. This is mere wishful thinking for an unproductive and lazy people. We need to re-engage and redirect our productive thoughts and begin to develop holistic strategies and programs that will ensure long-term economic grains.

For too long, we have been in the doldrums as a constituency without making any strides. Now, is the time to take corrective action and to make our constituency an example for others to follow. Our energies must never spent backbiting one another, but instead, elevating one another. We must be prepared to recondition our minds and to redirect and rededicate ourselves to the cause of humanity. This constituency group must provide the framework and the leadership to guide and direct creative and innovative energies. We can and must make a difference by changing our negative mentality and approaches. I ask you to read the program that you now hold in your hands. It reads and I quote: "Use the energy which would have been expended in those unproductive pursuits for improvement in one's own body, mind, and soul " Our society can be saved from moral, cultural, and spiritual decay by nurturing wholesome citizens from the cradle to the grave. This is the only way that we can truly achieve sustainable development and push our country forward.

We as members of this constituency have a moral and political responsibility to become committed to the principle of the SLP manifesto. We have a moral responsibility, each and every one of us, to do all we can on a personal, professional, and organizational level to share our skill, our expertise, our knowledge, and our wealth to ensure these principles become a reality.

As most of you know, I have been actively involved in this process for many, many years. Our lives are ruled by the politics of the country. You and I can make a meaningful contribution. As far back as fifteen to twenty years ago, I intimated my interest to enter the political life of the country. I was not able to

Ebb and Flow

do so because of my involvement in business at that time. As a young self-employed person, regrettably I did not see the need to go into active politics, until recently when I decided to run for the primary of the SLP, representing this constituency of Anse La Raye and Canaries. As you are aware, I was not successful in the primary, but continued to work along with the successful candidate and I am very happy that SLP now formed the government, following its landslide victory at the polls in May 1997. I would very much like, in the near future, to run for active politics again. I am however grateful for my appointment as a government senator in the Upper House. I look forward with great excitement and expectation to making further contributions in the senate.

I must applaud the efforts of the parliamentary representative for Anse La Raye/Canaries, Hon. Cyprian Lansiquot, for doing his best to provide effective representation on behalf of the people of this constituency. Mr. Lansiquot is relentless in his drive to improve this community. Several proposals have been submitted to cabinet on behalf of the constituency group aimed at making life much easier for the people of this community. I fully support him in his continued efforts. However, I do not wish to steal the thunder from Brother Cyprian Lansiquot, who will be addressing you momentarily on the many achievements and accomplishments in our constituency. Bravo Comrade Cyprian Lansiquot!

There is still a lot that must be done. You must bear in mind that the SLP remained in the political wilderness for well over thirty years. You know that Saint Lucians will never let you get away with making another political blunder. The SLP made this mistake in 1979, by engaging in a useless power struggle—and this blunder haunted the party. We in this constituency must never allow ourselves to be carried away by the petty internal wrangling to undermine the loyalty of members and our party leaders. We must renew our commitment and loyalty to our government and must trust the wisdom of their collective leadership. Today we should renew our commitment and to send a strong message to our detractors that we in this community are determined to stick together as brothers and sisters, and maintain the theme of our conference today: "Brotherhood and Service in the Community."

There is so much to be done. We have to reframe and reshape the thinking of community, our constituency, and our country. We must call on our party to provide the political awareness and education so as to ensure our continued commitment to our party. We have to change the total belief that our parliamentary representative can wave a magic stick and meet the needs of everyone

Political Speech

in our constituency at the same time. We must be patient and work with our representative to change the poor quality of life in our constituency. We as a constituency must be committed to ensuring that people can contribute meaningfully to the development of our community and our country.

As a constituency, we must start to assist in the reshaping of our community to think positively and together to develop strategies towards moving into the next century.

The SLP manifesto on page twenty-one defines its concept of community development. I quote: "When we say community development, we mean individuals, families, and government working together at the constituency level to define the priority needs to the community; each of them providing the levels of support that they can afford to address these needs and taking a common approach to solving their problems."

Therefore, politics must not be allowed to divide our people in warring factions, making the process counter productive and self-destructive. A country must always harness the creative energies of its people. No one political party in isolation can have all the human and financial resources needed to stimulate economic development for the benefit of the country as a whole. So we all must work together for the common good of Saint Lucia.

In closing, I urge the members of the Anse La Raye/Canaries Constituency Group to collectively energize and set out to create a community that is the envy of other communities in Saint Lucia. It is with regret that I now announce my decision not to seek re-election as chairman of this constituency group. Recent developments in my business and professional life have taken a serious toll on my family and myself. I need time to re-energize and to recuperate from mental and physical strain. Party work requires a certain level of commitment, focus, and organization such I cannot give at this present time.

However, I do believe there are others in our midst who are quite capable of carrying the mantle of leadership to the next critical stage of communal involvement and development. Know that you can count on me to continue to serve the constituency group in an ordinary capacity. I wish you every success in your future endeavour. As I know, with your support our party as well as our community will grow from strength to strength.

chapter thirty

TOURISM AND AGRICULTURE

In the following speech, I laid out a vision for the cooperation of the tourism and agriculture sectors: for the two to join forces so that Saint Lucia could see broad-based development across sectors.

Address by Noel N.S. Cadasse, President of the Saint Lucia Hotel and Tourism Association (SLHTA) at the Quarterly General Meeting on March 24, 1995

Ladies and gentlemen, let me take this opportunity to first welcome you to this, our first quarterly meeting of my presidency, and to invite you to participate fully in our deliberations here today. I hope that you will take this responsibility seriously, as the contribution and support of each one of you is vital for the proper development of our industry.

Since we last met, our task as decision makers has not been made any easier. In fact, some of the challenges that faced us then seem to have magnified tremendously, and as the industry takes on a global dimension, we need to position ourselves to respond promptly to the many opportunities that are available to us in every sector of our industry.

The competition in our industry is not only with our Caribbean neighbours but also with the world at large, and in most cases they have a similar product to offer. This has made it imperative that we mobilize our resources to create a tourism master plan. This plan must be geared towards the sustainability and long-term survival of the industry, and as members of a key organization in this important economic sector we must become more active and vigilant. We must therefore be in the forefront of planning and responding to the challenges ahead so as to maximize the benefits to our members and the industry as a whole.

Ebb and Flow

With the present crisis facing the banana industry, tourism is poised to be Saint Lucia's new economic saviour. Statistics indicate that this industry is the fastest growing sector of the economy with a steady annual growth rate of about 8 percent over the last five years. During the last year alone, the industry grew by a record 11.5 percent, thus eclipsing the previous record of the year before. If the trend continues, we may well see a new record again this year. Last year over 220,000 stay-over visitors came to Saint Lucia. This increase in growth and the potential for further increases in stay-over visitors demand that we move speedily to increase our existing stock of hotel rooms. Our present room capacity of approximately 3,000, with another 200 anticipated to become operational within the next year, may well prove to be grossly inadequate to handle the volume of visitors to Saint Lucia. Serious decisions will therefore have to be taken to address this need.

However, in considering plans for the advancement of the industry, we must not only look at the growth projections, but must also take time out to seriously address the factors that can inhibit the quality and competitiveness of our tourism product.

Training or the lack of it is one such factor, which we cannot ignore. We must continue to allocate resources to the education and training of our local employees so as to prepare them for positions of leadership in the industry. In this regard, I must commend Sandals Resorts and Club Saint Lucia for their outstanding efforts at training Saint Lucians for key positions in the industry. I would also like to thank the Organization of American States and the Caribbean Hotels Training Institute for their support and contributions to the training aspect of our industry. Our gratitude must also extend to the National Research and Development Foundation for its training projects, and we must also be thankful for the Hocking College Scholarship Program.

However, training of employees alone is not sufficient for our progress. We must focus on the training of entrepreneurs in the industry. As local investors and risk takers, our entrepreneurs need to equip themselves to participate successfully in the industry. Small hoteliers in particular must make the sacrifice to market their properties both individually and collectively. They need to undertake management-training courses, attend industry meetings, conferences and trade shows, so as to give them the guidance and direction to improve standards.

Our education and training thrust cannot be purely industry specific. It must also extend into other industries, particularly the agricultural industry, with which we must continue to develop greater linkages. This marriage

Tourism and Agriculture

between agriculture and tourism is of critical importance, not just to our industry but, to the economy as a whole. If the agricultural sector can fully satisfy the needs of the tourist industry, both in terms of fresh produce and processed or canned foods that would save the country millions of dollars in foreign exchange outflows, thus impacting positively on our balance of payment situation.

In addition, the organization of the agricultural sector to fulfill such a responsibility would mean that our dream of agricultural diversification for Saint Lucia would finally materialize. Moreover, the collaborative manner in which that dream would be pursued would eliminate the possibility of social upheaval and economic dislocation resulting from some inefficient farmers having to abandon banana production.

So it is critical that we come together as a strong force to lobby for our interests and to foster growth in the industry. We recognize that financial resources for significant long-term investments in the industry are not available locally. Government must therefore create the correct atmosphere that will encourage such capital to be brought into Saint Lucia. In this regard the proposed Hotel Incentives Bill must be piloted at a much faster pace. We need to see concrete policies in place, which will enable a developer to benefit from the incentives available as soon as he can satisfy the prescribed criteria and not after the matter is discussed at cabinet level. Special incentives must also be provided for the owners of small properties so as to allow them to grow and remain in business. We need to recognize them as providing a special service, which in many instances the larger hotels cannot provide, so we need to support them.

We also need to give some strong support to our taxi drivers, who have invested their lives in providing their vital services to our total industry. We note however, that their counterparts in the banana industry have been afforded greater incentives by way of duty-free concession on inputs and motor vehicles. We must recognize that the tourism industry is as much an export industry as the banana industry. Therefore, our taxi drivers should be granted similar concessions to those presently enjoyed by the banana farmers.

Ladies and gentlemen, we have to maintain the quality of our product at the very highest level. To do this, there are two other critical areas that must be addressed. These are, firstly, the protection of our environment, and secondly, the control of criminal acts against visitors. Our environment is probably our greatest asset. We need to cherish it, protect it, and keep it sacred. We cannot allow garbage to be dumped indiscriminately all over the place, our beaches to be mined illegally without regard to the effects on the industry, or waste to be dumped into our coastal reservoirs of rich marine life. The pollution and environmental degradation occurring in the world's large metropolitan cities have created a need in visitors to pursue countries offering a clean and healthy environment, and must give it to them or else they will look for it elsewhere.

On the matter of crime, my voice will continue to sound its clarion call. Every time I address you, I will call upon each and every one of you to denounce crime until the relevant authorities address this menace with the urgency it deserves. Our industry cannot afford the black listing of Saint Lucia because an upsurge in criminal activity. Crime is no longer on our beaches but it is now on every street in this country and approaching our doorsteps. The problem must be nipped in the bud, and government needs to take firm and decisive action in that regard. We note that they have moved in precisely that manner to deal with the problems in the banana industry which is poised to lead Saint Lucia in the twenty-first century, we have not been afforded the same level of importance, although we have been calling for action for some time now. The entire country must therefore be mobilized against this growing menace and we need to teach the criminals that crime doesn't pay.

The "Adopt-A-Farmer" Program has already indicated that there is great potential for farmers to supply the local tourism industry with fruits and vegetables. The program has received impressive reviews from several regional and international tourism publications, which have described it as "an innovative approach to sustainable tourism development." The Ministry of Agriculture must therefore take advantage of this marketing opportunity to strengthen the linkages between agriculture and tourism, which we spoke about earlier. We welcome the recent initiative taken by the Saint Lucia Marketing Board in organizing the recent AgriTour '95, which was aimed at reinstating dialogue and cooperation between the board and the hospitality industry.

However, we are concerned that the Fish Marketing Corporation, another sub-sector of the agricultural industry, continues to be a source of serious impediment and frustration to food and beverage managers in the hotel and restaurant business. As an island destination, people expect to have the option of fish and seafood offered on the local menu. In fact, our brochures promoting Saint Lucia give the visitor precisely that impression. However, the ridiculous prices set for such items as shrimp, lobster, and prime quality fish at the Fish Marketing Corporation ensure that the only way the visitor to Saint Lucia can enjoy seafood is in the pages of the brochure. The question is: why should the

Tourism and Agriculture

government want to be involved in the retailing of fish through a monopoly of the Fish Marketing Corporation? It is my view that if we allow the forces of free enterprise to operate in the fishing industry, I am positive that the prices of shrimp, lobster, and other exotic seafood will be such that the hotels and restaurants will then be able to offer these items on their menu.

Our approach to the development of the industry must be a collaborative one, in which all the key players are involved at the highest level. We must therefore continue to have dialogue with all the parties concerned from the vendors to the taxi drivers, to the farmers, to the unions, to the financial institutions, and all others involved. However, one such party we must work extremely close with is the airline industry. In recent months there has been a lot of uncertainty surrounding the availability of airline seats into Saint Lucia. BWIA, which in the past served us well, was considering reviewing their position on the European route due to restructuring. As a result, top-level negotiations had to be held with them to convince them that the service should continue. Negotiations are ongoing, and they have indicated that they are willing to put on three flights per week out of Miami and three per week from New York to Vigie Airport.

Attempts are still being made to encourage the BWIA to use the international airport at Vieux Fort, and hopefully they will be convinced of this in due course. In the meantime, we are pleased at the introduction of Carib Express, which is providing an additional service in the intra-regional sphere. We are also very thankful for the service provided by American Airlines presently, as the only scheduled carrier operating from North America. The charters which operate during the peak-season are also most welcomed and no effort must be spared in servicing the requirements of all these carriers.

Finally, ladies and gentlemen, it is my view that more attention should be directed towards the reduction of our seasonal variations in occupancy. Cultural tourism is an area that can play a critical role in this regard. Saint Lucia's rich cultural heritage must be used more resourcefully in the promotion of our island as a tourist destination. Our flower festivals, the La Rose and La Marguerite, must be promoted as a unique aspect of our tourism product. There is a need for us to offer more special events such as the Jazz Festival, which has become very successful in attracting visitors to the island. We hope that consideration will be given to the possibility of changing the scheduled date for Carnival and to use this special event as a marketing tool to attract more visitors to the island.

Ebb and Flow

And since we are on the question of marketing, I must emphasize the point that the Tourist Board must be given a realistic budget to carry out its mandate. If we are to maintain our place in the market, the Board must be given sufficient resources to market and promote the island. We note that the Bahamas, which is one of our major competitors, has a budget of US$44 million allocated to its tourism marketing effort. However, in Saint Lucia we are forced to work with a budget of under $2 million for actual marketing and promotion. How then can we guarantee that our market share will not be eroded by another Caribbean destination like the Bahamas, which not only offers a similar product but has the money to ensure that they receive the kind of attention they deserve in the marketplace?

In closing, let me take this opportunity to thank all of you for your support and encouragement during the last few months. My gratitude also goes out to the Executive Vice President for his loyalty and commitment. Special thanks also go out to the staff who has worked tirelessly to ensure this association remains the driving force in the industry. I hope that I can rely on the support of the board of directors and the general membership in helping to make our association stronger and stronger in 1995.

part three

PHOTOS

EBB AND FLOW

An anniversary dinner outing

Sons Ross & Kervin

Photos

Son Kervin

Father and Son, Noel and Ross

Daughters, left to right: Candace, Julianne, Cheryl-Anne

Daughter Candace, attorney-at-law

Photos

Daughters, left to right: Sharnelle, Juli-Anne, Liza

Son Ross, businessman

Ebb and Flow

Son Noel Jr., audio engineer, producer

Noel and daughters

Photos

Noel and family

Noel Cadasse

Family get together

Noel at the office

Photos

An evening with Noel and wife Julia

*Addressing Kiwanis
International Convention*

Business meeting in London, England. Left to right: St. Lucia Permanent Secretary (former), St. Lucia High Comissioner, London, England, St. Lucia Minister of Tourism (former), Noel Cadasse

Photos

Noel Addressing Association Conference

Opening address at Christmas dinner in Toronto

Desiderata

Go placidly amid the noise and haste, and remember what peace there may be in silence. As far as possible without surrender be on good terms with all persons. Speak your truth quietly and clearly; and listen to others, even the dull and ignorant; they too have their story. Avoid loud and aggressive persons, they are vexations to the spirit. If you compare yourself with others, you may become vain and bitter; for always there will be greater and lesser persons than yourself.

Enjoy your achievements as well as your plans. Keep interested in your career, however humble; it is a real possession in the changing fortunes of time. Exercise caution in your business affairs; for the world is full of trickery. But let this not blind you to what virtue there is; many persons strive for high ideals, and everywhere life is full of heroism.

Be yourself. Especially, do not feign affection. Neither be critical about love; for in the face of all aridity and disenchantment it is as perennial as the grass.

Take kindly the counsel of the years, gracefully surrendering the things of youth. Nurture strength of spirit to shield you in sudden misfortune. But do not distress yourself with imaginings. Many fears are born of fatigue and loneliness. Beyond a wholesome discipline, be gentle with yourself.

You are a child of the universe, no less than the trees and the stars; you have a right to be here. And whether or not it is clear to you, no doubt the universe is unfolding as it should.

Therefore be at peace with God, whatever you conceive Him to be, and whatever your labours and aspirations, in the noisy confusion of life keep peace with your soul. With all its sham, drudgery and broken dreams, it is still a beautiful world. Be careful. Strive to be happy.

—Max Ehrmann, 1927

CPSIA information can be obtained at www.ICGtesting.com
Printed in the USA
BVOW02s2007290815

415723BV00014B/384/P